HOUGHTON MIFFLIN HARCOURT

WRITE SOURCE

SkillsBook

TEACHER'S EDITION

Grade 7

GREAT
SOURCE®

 HOUGHTON MIFFLIN HARCOURT

A Few Words About the
Write Source SkillsBook

Grade 7

Before you begin . . .

The *SkillsBook* provides you with opportunities to practice the editing and proofreading skills presented in the Student Edition. That book contains guidelines, examples, and models to help you complete your work in the *SkillsBook*.

Each *SkillsBook* activity includes a brief introduction to the topic and examples illustrating how to complete that activity. You will be directed to the page numbers in the text for additional information and examples. The "Proofreading Activities" focus on punctuation and the mechanics of writing. The "Sentence Activities" provide practice in sentence combining and in correcting common sentence problems. The "Parts of Speech Activities" highlight each of the eight parts of speech.

The Next Step

Most activities include a **Next Step** at the end of the exercise. The purpose of the Next Step is to provide ideas for follow-up work that will help you apply what you have learned to your own writing.

Photo Acknowledgments   Cover (red coral) ©Photodisc/Getty Images; cover (blue/green coral) ©Digital Vision/Getty Images; cover (yellow coral), cover (bandanna) HMH Collection; cover (coral) ©Corbis; cover (light) ©Stockbyte/Getty; cover (bandanna triangle) Harcourt School Publishers.

Printed in the U.S.A.

ISBN   978-0-547-48446-4 (teacher's edition)

3 4 5 6 7 8   0928   15 14 13

4500398554   A B C D E F G

Table of Contents

Proofreading Activities

Sentence and Paragraph Activities

Parts of Speech Activities

Proofreading Activities

The activities in this section include sentences that need to be checked for mechanics, spelling, or correct word choice. Most of the activities also include helpful *Write Source* references. In addition, the **Next Step** activities encourage follow-up practice of certain skills.

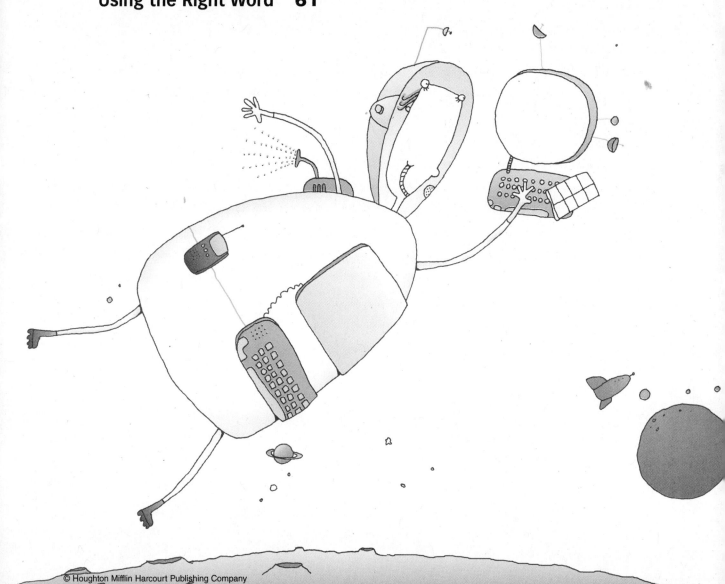

End Punctuation 1

Periods, exclamation points, and question marks signal the ends of sentences. At the same time, the end punctuation marks tell the reader what kind of thought is being expressed in each sentence. (See 579.1, 580.1, and 580.4 in *Write Source* for more information.)

Directions Put periods, question marks, and exclamation points where they are needed in the following paragraphs. Also supply the needed capital letters at the beginnings of sentences. The first sentence has been done for you.

1 Ants are amazing. **T**hey survived the extinction of the dinosaurs,

2 and now, millions of years later, there are more ants on the face of

3 the earth than any other creature.

4 The combined weight of all the ants in the world is about the

5 same as the combined weight of all living humans. **T**his is an incredible

6 fact since each ant weighs between 1 and 5 milligrams, or less than

7 one-millionth of a human's weight. **W**e are surrounded by 10 thousand

8 trillion of these creatures! **L**

9 Ants are everywhere. **L**arge-eyed ants dominate the rain forest

10 canopy, while other ants live deep underground. **A**ggressive army ants

11 move in formation to hunt and devour animals in their paths. **S**ome

12 ants take slaves. **O**ther ants actually tame species, such as aphids, and

13 feed off their secretions.

4

14   Ants prey upon and transport other insects and spiders into their

15 colonies, burying them and enriching the land they move far more turf

16 than earthworms, mixing vast quantities of nutrients into the soil.

17   Harvester ants alter the environment by transporting seeds into

18 their nests for food they decide which plants will succeed and which

19 will fail by tipping the balance in favor of the plants they prefer to eat.

20   Can you picture an ant gardening some ants create planting beds

21 out of soil, vegetable fibers, and other materials then they plant seeds

22 in the beds as the plants grow, ants feed on them the ant gardens of

23 Central and South America contain many plant species that cannot be

24 found anywhere else.

25   Two ant specialists, Bert Hölldobler and Edward Wilson, studied

26 ants for many years they asked themselves if there might be a good

27 reason for the success of ants they concluded, "Ants, like humans,

28 succeed because they 'talk' so well."

29   Ants talk by releasing substances that have as much meaning for

30 other ants as words have for people when ants in a colony

31 communicate, their companions cooperate instantly without the colony,

32 ants could not survive.

End Punctuation 2

Punctuation controls the movement of your writing. The end punctuation marks—periods, question marks, exclamation points—signal the end of a sentence and help the reader understand what you're trying to say in your writing. (See 579.1, 580.1, 580.4, and 600.1 in *Write Source* for rules and examples.)

Directions Place periods, question marks, and exclamation points where they are needed in the following narrative. Also, make sure the first word in each sentence is capitalized. The first two sentences have been done for you.

1   We arrived late in the night and pitched our tent in the dim light

2   cast by our camp lanterns. We went to bed with no idea where our

3   campsite was located.

4   The next morning, my little brother and I were up as soon as the

5   birds began to chatter. We slipped on our clothes and shoes, unzipped

6   the screen door, and stepped outside. The others were still nestled in

7   their sleeping bags. To our surprise, 100 yards from our door lay a

8   small lake. It was a deep green, even in the morning haze. On closer

9   inspection, we saw that the lake was covered with a thick blanket

10   of algae. At the shoreline, we picked up some rocks and tossed them

11   into the water. Wherever they landed, dark circles opened up and then

12   closed again.

13   The silence of the morning was broken only by the call of birds,

14   the dripping of trees, and the plops made by our high-arching rocks.

15 Suddenly, we heard a tremendous splash along the shore. we

16 wheeled around. "look at that" my brother shouted. algae was splattered

17 over a 20-foot circle, and ripples were spreading fast.

18   "No fish could have done that," I said.

19   "Maybe a big turtle" my brother shouted.

20   "Or somebody threw a log," I said. "except nobody else is here."

21   "Could it be a sea serpent" my brother whispered.

22   "There are no such things," I informed him.

23   "Oh no then what is that" he pointed to a line of humps moving

24 in the water far across the lake. i saw them, too. they moved, then

25 disappeared, then reappeared, and then disappeared again.

26   I wanted to believe in creatures like the Loch Ness monster. why

27 not my little brother believed with all his hear, but I felt too old for

28 that. I thought about schools of fish, diving birds, wheels falling from

29 airplanes, meteors from outer space—scientific sorts of things.

30   What made the splash I'll never know, but my brother and I will

31 never grow tired of telling the story of the monster in the lagoon—an

32 unsolved mystery in the history of our family camping trips.

Next Step Write a first draft about a mysterious or scary experience. Don't hold back. Let your reader share in the mystery and excitement. Try starting your story right in the middle of the action. Check your end punctuation when you finish.

Commas Between Items in a Series 1

Commas keep words and ideas from running together in a sentence. They are used between words, phrases, or clauses when there are three or more in a series. Read the following poem aloud.

> Without a comma at my command, more
>
>   punctuation I would demand.
>
> There'd be no brake to slow the rush, of cursor,
>
>   crayon, pen, or brush.
>
> My days of writing soon would end, without that modest little friend
>
> Who slips quietly in between, the words in series long or lean.

Now read it again to figure out where the missing commas should go. (See 582.1 in *Write Source* for more information.)

 Directions **Add commas to the series in the sentences below. The first sentence has been done for you.**

1. As we look back on the twentieth century, we should remember, think about, and try to learn from the events that shaped this remarkable period in history.

2. The United States fought in many conflicts during the twentieth century—among them World War I, World War II, the Korean conflict, the war in Vietnam, and the Gulf War.

3. Imagine life without antibiotics to fight infections, vaccinations to prevent diseases, or scanners to diagnose our illnesses.

4. In 1901, a visitor to a foreign city would have experienced strange new foods, clothing, and languages.

5. Today, in large cities throughout the world, you can find not only the native foods, dress, and language but also fast-food hamburgers, designer jeans, and the English language.

6. Do you think that your interests, hopes, fears, beliefs, and desires are formed partly by television, music, and movies?

7. Some countries try to ban foreign entertainment, censor radio and television broadcasts, destroy historical records, or jail protesting citizens in an attempt to control people's thoughts.

8. A history of the twentieth century will cover such topics as climate cycles, population growth, and urban sprawl.

9. People in the twentieth century created computers, radar, and penicillin, but they also gave the world hula hoops and foam cups.

10. In the first 25 years after the space age began, people orbited Earth, astronauts walked on the moon, and space probes studied the solar system.

11. When people study the last decade of the twentieth century, will they include baggy pants, nose rings, and colored hair as fads or major trends?

Next Step Choose the names of three of your classmates. Write two sentences including all three names. In the first sentence, use just the names themselves in a series. In the second sentence, include each of the names in a phrase or a clause about that person.

Commas Between Items in a Series 2

Commas keep words, phrases, and clauses in a series from running together. Understanding how to use commas is one of the best writing skills you can master. (For more information, see 582.1 in *Write Source*.)

 Directions Add commas to the following sentences. Then label the parts of the sentence you've punctuated by writing "W" for word, "P" for phrase, or "C" for clause. The first sentence has been done for you.

1. The U.S. National Park Service exists to protect places of special
   W *W* *W* *W*
   historical, cultural, scientific, or recreational interest.
   P

2. Kill Devil Hill (site of the Wright brothers' first flight), Manzanar
   P
   National Historic Site (where Japanese Americans were held during
   P
   World War II), and Cumberland National Historical Park (site of the
   Warrior's Path across the Appalachian Mountains) honor events in our
   nation's history.

3. Recreational parks, like Wolf Trap Farm Park for the Performing Arts,
   W *W* *W*
   offer art, music, and theater in a natural, outdoor setting.

4. Yellowstone, Glacier, Yosemite, and Acadia National Parks protect complex
   W *W* *W* *W*
   ecosystems that might otherwise be lost forever.

5. The increasing number of visitors places great demands on the parks,
   P *P*
   causing destruction of plant life, disruption of animal habitats, and
   P
   pollution of waterways.

6. Even the largest national parks cannot exist as islands in a sea of
   W *W* *W*
   houses, roads, and automobiles.

7. Some parks require thousands of acres because elk herds need to migrate *C*
from summer to winter pastures, wolves need to range over large *C*
territories to support their packs, and waterfowl need to move freely from *C*
one food source to another.

8. The Wilderness Act of 1964 is helping to save our parks by protecting *P*
primitive areas, re-creating natural habitat, and banning development. *P P*

> **Directions**
>
> Now it's your turn: Write a paragraph about a park or recreational area you have visited or heard about. Be sure to share what makes the place unique. Include at least one sentence with a series of words, phrases, or clauses.

_____

_____

_____

_____

_____

_____

_____

_____

Next Step All of the words or phrases you use in a series should be parallel—stated in the same way. Look over your paragraph. Have you used parallel forms in your sentences? Correct any words, phrases, or clauses that need to be changed. (See "Parallelism" on page 559 in *Write Source* for help.)

Other Comma Uses 1

If you want your writing to be clear and easy to understand, you will need to know how to use commas correctly. This activity will help you master three comma uses. (See page 582 in *Write Source* for more information.)

Examples

Commas Separate Items in a Series:
Michael Jordan, Scottie Pippen, and Tony Kukoc started for the Chicago Bulls in the 1997–98 season.

Commas After Introductory Words:
Yesterday, my brother and I watched the Bulls game on TV.

Commas Separate Units in a Number:
The Bulls had a sellout streak of 530 games at the 21,500-seat United Center.

Commas Separate Items in a Date or an Address:
On January 30, 1998, I watched the Bulls win at the United Center, which is located at 1901 W. Madison Street, Chicago, Illinois.

 Directions Using the rules described above as your guide, add commas as needed to the following sentences.

1. Scottie Pippen overcame back pain, a foot injury, and contract disputes to play an important part in the Bulls' sixth championship.

2. Scottie Pippen broke Magic Johnson's record of 1,724 all-time steals on February 21, 1998.

3. Now retired Michael Jordan collected 23 points, 8 assists, 6 rebounds, and 3 steals in the All-Star Game.

4. Please, can we go to Chicago, Illinois, to see the game against Seattle?

5. On February 12, 1999, we traveled to Chicago, Illinois, to see the game against Seattle.

6. My brother, mother, and three sisters are all Seattle basketball fans.

7. That night, the Chicago team shut down Seattle players Baker, Payton, and Schrempf.

8. More than 21,000 fans attended the game and consumed 14,378 hot dogs, 10,910 bags of peanuts, and 18,345 soft drinks.

9. This Chicago Bulls team will go down in history as one of the world's greatest after winning six championships in eight years.

10. The Bulls play in the United Center located at 1901 W. Madison Street, Chicago, Illinois.

11. In 1998, Michael Jordan's annual salary was $33,000,000, the average NBA player made $2,600,000, and the minimum salary was $272,250.

12. In his first 13 seasons, Michael Jordan played 35,887 minutes in 930 games and scored 29,277 points.

13. Unlike the NFL, the NHL, and major league baseball, the NBA had never lost a regular season game because of a labor disagreement until the 1998-99 season.

14. You can contact the commissioner by writing him at the National Basketball Association, 645 Fifth Avenue, New York, New York 10022.

Next Step Write a paragraph of 5 to 6 sentences describing your favorite team—either a professional team or one of your local teams. Try to write some sentences using the rules for commas covered in this exercise. Share your paragraph aloud with a classmate and check each other's work for the correct use of commas.

Other Comma Uses 2

Commas are like the dividers in your school binder. Just as a divider separates your math problems from your science notes, a comma helps you separate one clause or phrase from another, or one adjective from another. (For more information, see 584.1, 586.2, and 590.1 in *Write Source*.)

Examples

Commas Set Off Clauses:

Because Maria practices every day, she is a great snowboarder.
("Because Maria practices every day" is a dependent clause.)

Commas Set Off Phrases:

To compete in the Olympics, Maria must train for years.
("To compete in the Olympics" is an introductory phrase.)

Commas Separate Equal Adjectives:

Many young, athletic skiers are interested in snowboarding.
(The adjectives are *equal* because they could be written as "young" and "athletic.")

 Directions Add commas as necessary to the following sentences. The first sentence has been done for you.

1. Because snowboarding is easy to learn, it is very popular.

2. Although snowboarding is sometimes compared to skateboarding, snowboarding is more like surfing.

3. Yesterday, several snowboarders tried racing through icy, rutted snow.

4. If you are interested in trying snowboarding, you should get the right equipment.

5. After testing out lots of boards, Karlowe decided to get a freestyle board.

6. Because it is the shortest and widest of snowboards, the freestyle board makes tricks easier to do.

7. A *halfpipe* is a long, deep snow trench that snowboarders use to do flips and jumps.

8. Snowboards were invented by a creative East Coast surfer who got the idea by sliding over fresh, deep snow on a cafeteria tray.

9. Because snowboarders can get very wet and cold, they wear multiple layers of clothing.

10. Snowboarding can be done anywhere that skiing is done, except on flat cross-country trails.

11. Snowboarding equipment includes a freestyle or slalom board, bindings, and thick, chunky boots.

12. When first learning to snowboard, you have to decide to lead with your left foot or lead with your right.

13. If you catch the front or rear edge of your snowboard too deeply in the snow, you may crash.

14. After finding a great place to board, just strap yourself to the board and surf down the hill.

15. If you are excited about trying snowboarding, you can rent some basic used equipment and ride the nearest halfpipe.

Next Step In a paragraph, describe why you like (or don't like) snowboarding. Try to use introductory phrases and clauses in your writing. Remember to separate each introductory phrase or clause from the rest of the sentence with a comma. Read your paragraph aloud to a partner.

Commas to Set Off Nonrestrictive Phrases and Clauses 1

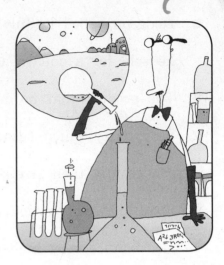

Let's practice punctuating **nonrestrictive** phrases and clauses, including appositives. The first step is to identify the phrase or clause as nonrestrictive—or unnecessary to the basic meaning of the sentence. The next step is to set off the nonrestrictive phrase or clause with commas. (Review the differences between restrictive and nonrestrictive below and also see 584.1 in *Write Source.*)

Examples

Restrictive:

The man who made Silly Putty became a millionaire.
(The information in the clause "who made Silly Putty" is needed to understand the sentence.)

Nonrestrictive:

Silly Putty, a glob of stretchy goo, was first called Nutty Putty.
(The information in the phrase "a glob of stretchy goo" is not needed to understand the sentence.)

 Directions Add commas as necessary to the following sentences. The first sentence has been done for you.

1. Silly Putty, originally known as Nutty Putty, was discovered in 1943 by James Wright.

2. James Wright, an engineer for General Electric, accidentally made Nutty Putty in his laboratory.

3. James Wright thought that Nutty Putty, which is made of boric acid and silicone oil, had no practical uses.

4. Peter Hodgson, an unemployed advertiser, found Nutty Putty in a toy store.

5. Hodgson called it Silly Putty and put it into small, plastic eggs that he sold for a dollar each.

6. The product that no one wanted made Hodgson a millionaire.

7. Silly Putty‸which became popular in the 1950s‸was pressed against comics and then stretched to make crazy impressions.

8. Soon kids who owned this stretchy goo realized that Silly Putty could also bounce very high.

9. In 1968, the astronauts who traveled on Apollo 8 carried Silly Putty into space to fight boredom and to fasten down tools during weightlessness.

10. In 1990, Binney and Smith Inc.‸the makers of Silly Putty‸added fluorescent colors.

11. Silly Putty‸which is now more than 50 years old‸is still a very popular toy.

12. A person who has a great imagination can think of new uses for ordinary products.

13. The Columbus Zoo‸which is in Ohio‸used Silly Putty to make plaster casts of gorillas' hands and feet.

Next Step Copy three sentences from this activity that contain a nonrestrictive phrase or clause. Then revise each sentence by crossing out the phrase or clause and substituting your own words. Be sure that the phrase or clause you add is nonrestrictive. Share your writing with a classmate.

Commas to Set Off Nonrestrictive Phrases and Clauses 2

Let's try punctuating more sentences that include restrictive and nonrestrictive information. Remember that nonrestrictive or unnecessary phrases and clauses are set off with commas, but restrictive phrases and clauses are not set off with commas. (For more information, see 584.1 in *Write Source*.)

 Directions   Add a comma before and after the nonrestrictive information. (Not all sentences need commas.) The first sentence has been done for you.

1. My youngest brother, Arturo, has a pet iguana named Felix.

2. Kids who want exotic pets must spend a lot of time learning how to take care of them.

3. Samir's parrot, Maurice, loves to mimic phone conversations and country singers.

4. The iguana that Joe owns eats both plants and animals.

5. The scarlet macaw, a popular pet, gets sick easily.

6. Cockatoos that mimic human speech are popular cage birds.

7. One of the largest cockatoos, the great palm, has black feathers and patches of bright red skin on its cheeks.

8. All cockatoos have feathered crests, which they can raise or flatten.

9. The tarantula, a long-legged, hairy spider, is found in warm areas.

10. Tarantulas use their big fangs to inject venom, which can be deadly, into their victims.

18

11. The miniature potbellied pig, one of the smartest exotic pets, is easy to train.

12. Pigs that wallow in the mud are trying to stay cool and to protect themselves from lice and other bugs.

13. The anaconda, a semiaquatic snake, is found in Central America and South America.

14. Anacondas, which eat birds and small animals, make unusual pets.

15. The giant anaconda that lives in our zoo is already 35 years old.

16. Levi wants to buy the boa that he saw advertised in the classified ads.

17. His mother, who is afraid of snakes, wants him to buy a macaw.

18. Most lizards, except the desert iguana, sleep during the hottest part of the day.

19. Exotic pets that are well cared for may live for many years.

20. Every year veterinarians must find new homes for exotic pets that have become too big or too dangerous for their owners.

21. Kids who want exotic pets must remember that these pets require a lot of care.

22. Owning an anaconda or a black widow spider, both dangerous animals, is not a good idea.

Next Step Write three sentences of your own that contain nonrestrictive information. Ask a classmate to place the commas in the correct places. Try to stump your classmate with creative sentences. After your partner has finished, read the sentences aloud.

Commas with Interruptions, Direct Address, and Interjections

Commas sometimes separate the unnecessary parts of sentences from the necessary parts. For example, when a word or phrase or clause is not necessary to the basic meaning of a sentence, that word or phrase or clause is separated from the rest of the sentence by a comma or by commas. **Interruptions, nouns of direct address**, or **interjections** are considered nonessential and are separated from the main sentence with commas. (For more information, see 584.3, 588.2, and 588.3 in *Write Source*.)

Examples

"Didn't you swim with dolphins, Hillary?"
"Yeah, I also swam near a shark, believe it or not, off the Florida Keys."

 Directions Add commas wherever they are needed in the sentences that follow. The first sentence has been done for you.

1. Of course, just the thought of a shark, as we all know, sends shivers down most swimmers' spines.

2. Contrary to popular belief, though, sharks rarely attack people.

3. "Simply stated, Bill, humans have not swum in the oceans long enough for sharks to adapt to hunting humans."

4. Many myths, most of them untrue, have developed about sharks.

5. Some people think, even though it's not true, that sharks must swim continuously so that they don't sink.

6. Not surprisingly, this belief is based on the fact that, unlike other fish, sharks do not have a swim bladder filled with air to help them stay afloat in the water.

7. A shark's huge liver, almost 75 percent of its body weight, contains enough fat to make the fish float.

8. Without a fish's air-filled swim bladder, you see, deepwater sharks can move rapidly from the depths to the surface without decompressing.

9. Sharks, unchanged in the last 70 million years, are seldom seen in fossils.

10. Fossils are rare, unfortunately, because sharks have skeletons made of cartilage, like the framework of your nose and ears, instead of bone.

11. Some baby sharks are born live while others hatch from eggs deposited in pods known, believe it or not, as "mermaids' purses."

12. Just imagine, sharks must grow for about 15 years before they are mature enough to reproduce.

13. "Yes, Jamal, sharks need protection since they are being killed more quickly than they can replace themselves."

Next Step Write a letter to send to your local newspaper, or to share with your class, about a topic you know or care about. Remember to check your facts before sending or sharing your letter.

Commas to Set Off Explanatory and Appositive Phrases

Commas are used to set off explanatory phrases from the rest of the sentence. Explanatory, or nonrestrictive, phrases contain information that is *not* necessary to the basic meaning of the sentence. That's why they are set off by commas. (For more information, see 586.1 and 588.4 in *Write Source*.)

Examples

Commas Set Off Explanatory Phrases:
The Grand Canyon, <u>located in northwestern Arizona</u>, is an incredible place.

Commas Set Off Nonrestrictive Appositive Phrases:
Bob, my classmate, visited the Grand Canyon.

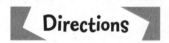 **Directions**   Add commas to the following sentences as needed. The first sentence has been done for you.

1. Bob and Paola, Bob's neighbor, took a trip to the Grand Canyon last summer.

2. The Grand Canyon, which contains buttes, mesas, and valleys, is an awesome place to visit.

3. The boys rented burros, small donkeys, to use when traveling down the trails to the bottom of the canyon.

4. Their guide, Raoul, warned them that they should dress in layers because the temperature changes quickly in the canyon.

5. The temperature at the bottom of the canyon, even in the fall, can be very warm.

6. The two friends, both camping fanatics, wanted to set up camp at the bottom of the canyon.

7. They carried supplies, including tents and sleeping bags, on the backs of their burros.

8. Bob's parents, Phil and Maria Magrath, stayed at the top of the canyon.

9. The parents agreed, after a lot of persuading, to let the boys join a camping group headed to the bottom of the canyon.

10. The camping trip, four days and three nights, was one the boys will never forget.

11. The campers left from the canyon's south rim, 7,000 feet above sea level, and rode their burros down the steep trail.

12. The boys' burros, named Pancho and Cisco, were very surefooted on the narrow trail that wound 5,000 feet down to the Colorado River.

13. The boys had to keep their burros very close together, and sometimes the burros, letting others pass, stepped right near the edge of the trail.

14. Temperatures reached 100° F, which is 38° C, so the boys had to drink a gallon of water each day to avoid dehydrating.

15. The boys were on the lookout for a special type of snake, the Grand Canyon rattlesnake, that blends into the canyon's pink sandstone.

Next Step Think about a park or campsite that you know well, and imagine camping there with a friend. Then write a paragraph or two describing your experience. Ask a classmate to check your writing for correct comma usage. Then share your writing with the class.

Commas in Compound Sentences

One way to join two independent clauses is to connect them with a comma and a coordinating conjunction (*and, but, or, nor, for, so, yet*). Knowing that you can combine simple sentences in this way will help you to edit more effectively. Also, using this technique will help you to create smoother transitions and more interesting sentences. (See 590.2 in *Write Source* for more information.)

 Directions Combine each of the following groups of sentences by using a comma and a coordinating conjunction. Avoid creating comma splices, which result from combining two sentences without a conjunction. The first sentence has been done for you.

1. Blue whales are the largest living creatures. Tortoises have the longest life span.

   Blue whales are the largest living creatures, but tortoises have the

   longest life span.

2. Some swifts and falcons can travel at more than 200 miles per hour. Only hummingbirds can fly backward.

   Some swifts and falcons can travel at more than 200 miles per hour,

   but [(or) yet] only hummingbirds can fly backward.

3. Amazon ants are fierce. Fire ants are even fiercer and have been known to sting birds and other larger animals.

   Amazon ants are fierce, yet [(or) but] fire ants are even fiercer and

   have been known to sting birds and other larger animals.

4. Most mammals see color as shades of gray. Some apes and monkeys see all the colors.

   Most mammals see color as shades of gray, but [(or) yet] some

   apes and monkeys see all the colors.

5. A centipede should have 100 legs, according to its name. Some centipedes have more than 250 pairs of legs.

A centipede should have 100 legs, according to its name, yet some

centipedes have more than 250 pairs of legs.

6. Mammals have red blood. Insects have yellow blood.

Mammals have red blood, and insects have yellow blood.

7. Dogs can produce about 10 different sounds. Cats can produce more than 100 vocal sounds.

Dogs can produce about 10 different sounds, but cats can produce

more than 100 vocal sounds.

8. An owl cannot move its eyes. An owl must move its whole head to look in different directions.

An owl cannot move its eyes, so it must move its whole head to look

in different directions.

9. Elephant seals can stay underwater for 30 minutes. They can dive to depths of more than 500 feet.

Elephant seals can stay underwater for 30 minutes, and they can

dive to depths of more than 500 feet.

Next Step Write a paragraph about a particular type of plant or animal that interests you. Try to use several compound sentences in your writing. Share your paragraph with a classmate.

Comma Rules

Of all of the punctuation marks, the one that has the most uses—and probably causes the most confusion—is the comma. *Write Source* covers many different rules for using commas. (For more information see pages 582–590 in *Write Source*.)

 Directions — Place commas correctly in each sample sentence. Then write the rule that applies to the comma usage. Use *Write Source* to do this exercise. The first sentence has been done for you.

1. My favorite foods are hamburgers, french fries, and pizza.

Rule: _Commas are used between words, phrases, or clauses in a series._

2. Mom must have told me at least 1,0 0 0,0 0 1 times to improve my diet.

Rule: _Commas are used to distinguish hundreds, thousands, millions, and so on, in numbers._

3. On February 1, 2004, we will be moving to Boston, Massachusetts.

Rule: _Commas are used to distinguish items in a date and items in an address._

4. "I'm sure," said Dad, "that Boston has some good pizza parlors."

Rule: _Commas are used to set off the exact words of the speaker from the rest of the sentence._

5. We can't, however, stay very long.

Rule: _Commas are used to set off a word, phrase, or clause that interrupts the main thought of a sentence._

6. Yes, we'll be there on time.

Rule: Commas are used to separate an interjection or a weak exclamation from the rest of the sentence.

7. Dad, is that all you think I'm worried about?

Rule: Commas are used to separate a noun of direct address from the rest of the sentence.

8. The two friends love to go golfing, and they are working to qualify for the state tournament next year.

Rule: A comma may be used between two independent clauses that are joined by a coordinating conjunction.

9. My uncle beamed as he took hold of the large, shining trophy.

Rule: Commas are used to separate two or more adjectives that equally modify the same noun.

10. My uncle, an expert angler, won the fishing contest.

Rule: Commas should separate an explanatory phrase (or a nonrestrictive appositive) from the rest of the sentence.

11. Uncle Josh, who had traveled 600 miles to participate, was very glad he had entered the fishing contest.

Rule: Commas are used to punctuate nonrestrictive phrases and clauses (those phrases or clauses that are not necessary to the basic meaning of the sentence).

Comma Review

| **Directions** | After reviewing the comma rules in the previous exercises, place commas correctly in the following sentences. (See pages 582–590 in *Write Source* for more information.) |

1. A group of geese is a *gaggle*, but it is more commonly called a flock.

2. A *clip joint* is a shop, store, or other place of business where customers are overcharged.

3. *Acrophobia* is the fear of heights, *claustrophobia* is the fear of enclosed spaces, and *hydrophobia* is the fear of water.

4. Abraham Lincoln was born on February 12, 1809, on a farm near Hodgenville, Kentucky.

5. Mr. Lincoln served as president of the United States from March 4, 1861, to April 15, 1865.

6. On June 3, 1979, more than 140,000,000 gallons of oil spilled from an oil well in the Gulf of Mexico.

7. Mark's new address is 310 Greens Drive, Boston, Massachusetts 02109.

8. Send your requests to the *Daily Post*, 211 Main Street, Willowlane, Missouri 64402.

9. "Did you know," asked Dan, "that London Bridge is no longer in London?"

10. "Sue, these are my parents."

11. Mr. Dobson, our English teacher, is out with the flu.

12. Sliding into first base, I scraped my elbow raw.

Directions Place commas correctly in the following sentences. (Refer to pages 582–590 in *Write Source* if necessary.)

1. "Dad, here are the good seats we've been telling you about."

2. "Wow," said Chris, "these are great!"

3. The usher, a young man with a beard, heard him and smiled.

4. Dad took orders and went to get sodas, popcorn, and pretzels.

5. The attendance, by the way, turned out to be more than 42,000.

6. The names and locations of Caroline Adams, M.D., and Samuel Cline, M.D., were posted on signs near the stage in case of emergencies.

7. We saw Miss Daniels, our neighbor, at the concert.

8. The music, which sounded perfect from our seats, carried out to the far ends of the stadium.

9. The concert was fantastic, and the crowd, loving it, clapped and screamed loudly.

10. Boy, it was hard to believe I would enjoy the same music as my grandpa, a teenager in the '70s.

11. For a bunch of old guys, the band called the Rolling Stones really rocked.

12. Everybody loved it when Mick Jagger, the Stones' lead singer, strutted across the stage.

13. The Stones' encore included "As Tears Go By," "Angie," and "Get Off Of My Cloud," but they didn't play "Ruby Tuesday."

14. "This concert was a lot mellower than the Stones' concert at Altamont on December 6, 1969," Grandpa said.

Semicolons and Colons

A **semicolon** is sometimes used in place of a period or in place of a comma and a conjunction. A semicolon signals that the ideas in the two independent clauses are similar in thought or in style. (*He came; he conquered.*)

A **colon,** on the other hand, mainly calls the readers' attention to what comes after the colon, whether it be a list or a key word. (For more information, see pages 594 and 596 in *Write Source.*)

Examples

Semicolons Join Independent Clauses:
My brother listens to punk rock; I listen to country music.
(Instead of a comma and a conjunction, a semicolon joins the two independent clauses.)

Semicolons Join Independent Clauses Connected by a Conjunctive Adverb:
Margarita listens to the Beatles; however, she also likes jazz music.
(A semicolon joins the two independent clauses with the conjunctive adverb "however.")

Colons Introduce a List:
Motown Records has recorded many great artists: Stevie Wonder, Diana Ross, Smokie Robinson, the Temptations, and the Four Tops.

Colons Separate a Word for Emphasis:
Most record companies are motivated by the same thing: money.

 Directions Add semicolons and colons to the following sentences as needed. The first sentence has been done for you.

1. My friends and I want to start our own band; however, we can't agree on a name for it.

2. I think the name Purple Watermelons is cool; Yuri thinks that it's too weird.

3. Our band wants to get some experience playing in public; as a result, we're willing to play anywhere.

4. We play many different kinds of music; however, we don't play anything very well.

5. My mom thinks there's only one word to describe our band: loud.

6. Umberto plays the following instruments: saxophone, guitar, trumpet, electric bass, synthesizer, and drums.

7. Last week we played at the Summerdale Senior Center; they didn't like our music.

8. We try to play all kinds of music: folk, punk, rap, and country.

9. There is one thing that separates good bands from poor ones: practice.

10. My friends and I dream of recording a hit song; we want to be big stars.

11. We practice in our garage; many famous musicians started out by playing in unique places: garages, attics, churches, and parks.

12. We experiment with new styles; we have a country-pop song, a folk-punk song, and a swing-rock song.

13. Our best gig so far was the kindergarten graduation; we really had those kids rocking.

14. If we do become stars, there are many things I want to do: buy a car, meet other stars, and get our band's picture on the cover of *Rolling Stone*.

15. We even have the title of our first album picked out: *Fame*.

Next Step Write a paragraph about a dream you have for your future—what you hope to do when you are an adult. Describe that dream in a paragraph using the rules for semicolons and colons. Share your writing aloud with a classmate.

Punctuating Dialogue

Talking is so easy that you don't have to think about it. You just . . . talk. But recording "talk" on paper is another matter entirely—one that can be a lot of work. There are definite rules to follow regarding the use of quotation marks, commas, end marks, and capital letters. (See 598.1 and 600.1 in *Write Source* for more information.)

Example

"**When will we leave for camp?**" **asked Todd.**
(The *question mark* is placed inside the quotation marks because the quotation is a question.)

 Directions — Punctuate the following dialogue with quotation marks, commas, and end marks. The first sentence has been done for you.

1   "All aboard, Scouts," said Counselor Dave as he climbed into the

2   bus. "Are you men prepared to camp in the Sonora Desert tonight?"

3   "Not yet, Dave," shouted Andy. "We still need to buy some sandpaper!"

4   "Why do you need sandpaper?" asked the puzzled counselor.

5   Andy grinned. "We're going to need a map when we drive through

6   the desert."

7   As the bus pulled up to the campground, Counselor Dave shouted,

8   "The last man off this bus is a rotten egg!"

9   "Excuse me, Counselor," said Andy. "I can't get down off the bus."

10   "Why not?" asked the counselor. "What is the problem?"

11   "Everyone knows you can only get *down* from a goose," (or) . Andy

12   laughed.

13 The next morning Counselor Dave rubbed his aching back and

14 yawned. I didn't sleep a wink in my tent, so I traded with Counselor

15 Ted. His tent wasn't any better.

16 Andy laughed and said, No wonder. You were just too tense, trying

17 to sleep in two tents.

_____

_____

_____

_____

_____

_____

_____

_____

_____

_____

_____

Next Step In the space above, write a short dialogue with a partner. Take turns writing, just as if you were talking.

Quotation Marks and Italics

Quotation marks are used to punctuate titles of shorter works. Titles of longer works are italicized. (If you are handwriting the title of a longer work, you should underline it.) For more information about italics and quotation marks, refer to 600.3 and 602.3 in *Write Source*.

Directions | Punctuate the following sentences. Remember that periods and commas are always placed inside quotation marks. The first sentence has been done for you.

1. In the <u>Utne Reader</u> magazine article "How to Future-Proof Your Life," the author says you should pack lightly.

2. A burglary at the Watergate Hotel in Washington, D.C., was reported in the <u>Washington Post</u> and recorded in the book <u>All the President's Men</u>.

3. Two books I like are <u>Are You My Mother?</u> and <u>The Cat in the Hat</u>.

4. As <u>Titanic</u> was sinking, the band played "Nearer, My God, to Thee."

5. A moving song, "The Circle of Life," from the movie <u>The Lion King</u> is inspired by African drumming.

6. Online magazines, or interactive magazines, such as <u>Digital Animators</u>, appeal to readers who would rather surf the Internet than browse through libraries.

7. Melville's novel <u>Moby Dick</u> is famous for its whaling lore, such as the chapter titled "Scrimshander."

8. Please turn up the volume so we can hear the song "Octopus's Garden."

9. Our faithful retriever wouldn't bring in the newspaper because the banner headline read "Man Bites Dog."

10. In 1963, John Glenn blasted into space in Friendship 7, and 35 years later, he returned to space aboard the space shuttle Discovery.

11. Sherlock Holmes utters the classic line, "By Jove, Watson, I've got it!" in "The Adventure of Charles August Milverton," a story from the book The Return of Sherlock Holmes.

12. "When You Say Nothing at All" was a big hit for Alison Krauss from her Alison Krauss and Union Station Live CD.

13. Many newspapers, including the New York Times, Chicago Tribune, and San Jose Mercury News, have their own Web sites.

14. Humphrey Bogart never said, "Play it again, Sam," in the movie Casablanca, a film based on a play called Everybody Comes to Rick's.

15. The school newspaper, the Yorkville Yacker, reviewed the movie Finding Nemo in an article entitled "Fishy Fun."

16. The musical group Chicago, the musical play Chicago, and the poem "Chicago" by Robert Frost are all named after the Illinois city.

Next Step On your own paper, write three sentences. In the first sentence, include the title of a song. In the second one, include the title of a poem, and in the third one, include the title of an article in a newspaper. When you have finished, check your work to be sure you have used italics and quotation marks correctly.

Italics and Parentheses

Italics are like flashing lights. They catch your attention right away because they look different than the regular type on the page. Italics alert readers to titles, foreign words, and words that are being used in a special way.

Parentheses separate words or phrases added to a sentence to make it clearer. They are really a lot like commas and dashes because they help prevent ideas from getting jumbled together. We use parentheses instead of commas and dashes when we want less emphasis on the separated material. (*Write Source* explains the uses of italics and parentheses in more detail at 602.3–602.5 and 612.4.)

Examples

Italics in Titles:
The River is one of my favorite adventure books.

Italics for Foreign Words:
Orcinus orca is the Latin name for killer whale.

Italics for Special Uses:
Try to say *rubber baby buggy bumpers* five times fast.

Parentheses for Added Information:
The author (Gary Paulsen) is a favorite of kids.

 Directions Add underlining (for italics) or parentheses to the following sentences. The first sentence has been done for you.

1. I have such a hard time saying the word <u>minimum</u>.

2. S. E. Hinton wrote <u>The Outsiders</u> when she was 16 years old.

3. The article on skydiving was in last month's issue of <u>Sports Illustrated</u>.

4. Our house in Grand Marais (actually the north shore of Lake Superior) is really a cabin.

5. This winter I saw <u>Lord of the Rings: The Return of the King</u> at a movie theater downtown.

36

6. The Latin name for one of the largest dinosaurs is Tyrannosaurus Rex.

7. Everyone thought Titanic was an unsinkable ship.

8. The New York Times published an article about kids starting their own businesses.

9. What is the French word for love?

10. How many i's are there in the word Mississippi?

11. You should order at least six dozen (72) barbecue buns for the party.

12. The tongue twister Peter Piper is harder to say than the tongue twister she sells seashells.

13. With his new braces, Paul found it hard to say s's and th's.

14. He rode his bike (actually a moped) back and forth to school.

15. Have you read The Hatchet, another book by Gary Paulsen?

16. If you switch the letters r and d in the word read, you get dear.

17. Parentheses (those curvy brackets) are always used in a pair to set off words in a sentence.

18. CD's (compact discs) replaced magnetic tapes as the main format for storing recorded music.

19. The Spanish word hola and the Italian phrase buòn giorno mean the same thing (hello).

Next Step Write a paragraph about your favorite book or movie. Describe it using details that would convince someone else to read the book or see the movie you are describing. What made that book or movie really interesting? Use italics and parentheses whenever necessary in this paragraph. Share your paragraph with the class.

Apostrophes 1

Apostrophes are used to form contractions and to show ownership or possession. (See 604.1, 604.4, and 606.1–606.4 in *Write Source* for more information about apostrophes.)

Examples

To Form Contractions:
Wouldn't riding a unicycle be fun?
(would + not = wouldn't)

To Show Possession:
A unicycle's wheel is small.

> **Directions** For each of the underlined words below, write "C" if an apostrophe is used correctly, add apostrophes to the words that need them, and correct any misplaced apostrophes. The first two sentences have been done for you.

1 Paula loves to ride her friend's [C] unicycle. She didn't take

2 long to learn, and she doesnt [doesn't] worry about falling. A unicycle is

3 recognized easily by it's [its] single wheel. Paula's [C] friend received his unicycle

4 from his brother-in-law; its [C] seat is mounted on a pole 20 feet high.

5 Naturally, a unicycles' [unicycle's] pedals must be up near the seat. Paula's [C] friend's [C]

6 vehicle is not your usual, run-of-the-mill unicycle. Pumping a unicycle is

7 hard, sweaty work, so theres [there's] a fan installed on the 20-foot pole with a

8 generator attached to the wheel's [C] hub. Isn't [C] Paula's [C] friends' [friend's] riding

9 machine a sight to see? Now they cant [can't] wait to try out the

10 brother's-in-law [brother-in-law's] new toy—a *miniature* unicycle.

Apostrophes 2

By now, you know that apostrophes are used to form contractions and to show possession, but they can do other things, too. In this activity, you'll discover some other ways you can use apostrophes. (See 604.2, 604.3, and 606.5 in *Write Source* for more information.)

Examples

In Place of Omitted Letters or Numbers:
In the summer of '98, we rode 16 rockin' roller coasters.

To Form Plurals:
Be sure to cross your t's and dot your i's.

To Express Time or Amount:
My dad took a week's vacation so that he could come with us.

> **Directions** Add at least one apostrophe to each of the following sentences. You will need to form contractions in some sentences.

1. Marcel ~~could not~~ couldn't wait to ride the Son of Beast, the fastest wooden roller coaster in the world.

2. He saved a month's worth of allowance for the class of '05 trip.

3. The figure 8's on this roller coaster made it especially scary.

4. Lionel ~~does not~~ doesn't know whether he should try the Hercules or Batman.

5. It's hard to imagine that either could be scarier than the Desperado.

6. People sat in rows of 2's and 3's in the hanging roller coaster.

7. Tomorrow's rides will be even more amazing than today's rides.

8. ~~They will~~ They'll be faster, bigger, and more daring.

9. Who's going to be brave enough to try these new roller coasters?

Next Step Write a first draft of a story about a special vehicle in your life. Make sure that you use apostrophes correctly in your writing. Share your results.

Apostrophes 3

Apostrophes can be used in your writing to show possession—to say, "Hey, that belongs to me!" (See 604.4 and 606.1–606.4 in *Write Source* for more details about how to use apostrophes to show possession.)

Examples

Singular Possessives:
Cedar Point's **Mean Streak roller coaster is one of the world's longest wooden coasters.**

Plural Possessives:
The visitors' **hearts raced as they plunged down the coaster hills.**

Shared Possession:
Latoya, Eli, and Gabriel's **favorite roller coaster is the Wild Thing at Valleyfair.**
Latoya's, Eli's, **and** Gabriel's **favorite snacks are different.**

Possessives in Compound Nouns:
My sister-in-law's **biggest fear is falling out of a roller coaster.**

Possessives with Indefinite Pronouns:
Everyone's **hands grab the safety bar during loops.**

Directions | In the following sentences, add an apostrophe where needed to show possession. But be careful—not every sentence needs an apostrophe. The first sentence has been done for you.

1. The earliest roller coasters tracks were made from cut lumber and tree trunks.

2. The first roller coasters were made in Russia in the fifteenth century.

3. Childrens lives were often in danger on those early roller coasters.

4. The worlds first hanging roller coaster appeared in 1981 in Cincinnati, Ohio.

5. In July 2003, the worlds tallest and fastest hanging roller coaster was the Top Thrill Dragster.

6. The Top Thrill Dragster's fastest speed is 120 miles per hour.

7. Its features include diving loops, rolls, and high-speed spirals.

8. My sister-in-law's scariest ride was on the Thunder Run at Kentucky's Six Flags.

9. Roller coasters' safety rules protect the lives of their passengers.

10. Jacco's, Ruth's, and Tobie's families spend the summer going from one amusement park to the next.

11. The world's first thrill ride to reach 100 miles per hour was Dreamworld's Tower of Terror.

12. The 8,133-foot Steel Dragon 2000 is Japan's longest steel roller coaster.

13. The Beast is everyone's favorite wooden roller coaster.

14. This year's most popular roller coaster was the Desperado at Buffalo Bill's Resort in Nevada.

15. The country's first steel roller coaster was Disneyland's Matterhorn Mountain, which opened in 1959.

16. Coney Island's Wonder Wheel combines a Ferris wheel's circular path with a roller coaster's thrills.

17. Our family rated ten roller coasters, and my two brothers' top choice was Apollo's Chariot.

Next Step In a paragraph describe your favorite amusement park ride. Ask a classmate to check your writing for correct use of possessive apostrophes.

Hyphens

Hyphens can be used to divide words at the end of a line and to form compound words. It might seem that hyphens have two opposite purposes; but really, hyphens have a single purpose: to make your writing clearer. (Refer to 608.2–608.4 and 610.2 in *Write Source* for more information.)

Examples

To Make a Compound Word:
My thirteen-year-old sister is very good at Frisbee golf.

To Create New Words:
The self-taught musician started his own band.

Between Numbers in a Fraction or a Compound Number:
Would twenty-two people each drink one-half cup of eggnog?

To Join Letters and Words:
The boomerang, a V-shaped stick, was sold by Wham-O Manufacturing.

 Directions Add hyphens to the following sentences as needed. The first sentence has been done for you.

1. My brother-in-law owns nine Frisbees and thirty-two hula hoops.

2. My great-uncle was a friend of the Frisbee's inventors.

3. These self-employed inventors also created popular toys like boomerangs and slingshots.

4. Many ever-popular products were made by long-forgotten inventors.

5. The can opener was invented in 1858, but a more user-friendly version was made in 1870.

6. Blue jeans, the all-American pants, were invented by a canvas salesperson from San Francisco during the gold rush of the 1850s.

7. By inventing these basic all⟨around pants, Levi Strauss created a new industry.

8. Blue jeans, now a world⟨famous product, were first made out of canvas.

9. In 1916, Garrett Augustus Morgan was given a medal for his safety⟨hood invention, which led to the development of the gas mask.

10. Use of the just⟨invented gas mask saved the lives of three⟨fourths of the workers in a tunnel explosion that year.

11. One of the ex⟨directors of the American Red Cross was Dr. Charles Drew.

12. Out⟨of⟨work people sometimes become great inventors.

13. One of the most well⟨known inventors was Alexander Graham Bell.

14. It took many years of trial⟨and⟨error research to invent the X⟨ray machine.

15. Forty⟨one out of sixty⟨eight people agreed that most inventions are made from one⟨tenth inspiration and nine⟨tenths perspiration.

16. If you have an idea for a super⟨duper invention, you could possibly become a self⟨made millionaire.

Next Step Invent a game that you could play with an everyday product found in your home. Then write a paragraph or two explaining how to play the game. Check your writing for correct use of hyphens. Share your writing aloud with a classmate.

Hyphens and Dashes

Hyphens connect words, numbers, and letters.

Dashes can add interruptions, information, or emphasis to your writing. Though dashes can be an effective writing tool, don't overuse them! (See pages 608, 610, and 612.1–612.3 in *Write Source* for more about dashes and hyphens.)

Examples

Hyphens:

Being a juggler isn't an average nine-to-five **job.**
(The hyphens turn the words "nine to five" into a single-thought adjective.)

Dashes:

Look out—that puddle is two feet deep!
(The dash and following text add emphasis and information to the warning.)

 Directions Punctuate the following sentences correctly. The first sentence has been done for you.

1. That's not your run-of-the-mill slam dunk.

2. Your brother-in-law really knows how to fix cars.

3. My great-grandfather is 99 today.

4. There's only one sport—swimming—I've ever really enjoyed.

5. Can we make a U-turn and go back to that gas station?

6. No one—and I mean no one—may leave this room.

7. Ann slipped on the ice-covered sidewalk—an accident waiting to happen.

8. Arlo Hale is the president-elect of the Nottingham Running Club.

Next Step Write three sentences about your favorite school subject. Try to use at least one hyphen and one dash. Read your sentences aloud to a partner.

Dashes

Dashes set off parts of a sentence or show a sudden break in the flow of a sentence. They create pauses in your writing that are a bit stronger and more dramatic than comma pauses. Use them sparingly in formal writing. (See 612.1–612.3 in *Write Source* for more information.)

Examples

To Indicate a Sudden Break:
Never —and I mean never —has a toy sold as well as the hula hoop.

To Emphasize a Certain Word, a Series of Words, a Phrase, or a Clause:
The hula hoop —an Australian invention —was first sold in the United States.

To Indicate Interrupted Speech:
I wanted to tell you that —well, that —I lost your hula hoop.

Directions ▷ Add dashes to the following sentences as needed. The first sentence has been done for you.

1. Both Frisbees and hula hoops were popular⟨very popular⟩in the 1950s.

2. Frisbees, Silly Putty, yo-yos⟨all of these have become classic toys.

3. The first hula hoops cost only $1.98⟨an unbelievable bargain!

4. Between 60 and 100 million hula hoops⟨an incredible number⟩were sold in just a few months.

5. Last week⟨no, let me see⟨was it⟨yes, last week⟨I bought a hula hoop.

6. The hula hoop was named after a very popular Hawaiian dance⟨the hula.

7. In the 1940s, students at Yale University tossed around pie platters from the local bakery⟨William R. Frisbie's Bakery⟨between classes.

8. The students were never⟨as you might imagine⟨given credit for their invention.

Punctuation Review 1

Directions Proofread the paragraphs below. Draw a line through any mark of punctuation or word that is used incorrectly; add any needed punctuation or capital letters. (For more information see pages 579–612 in *Write Source*.) The first two sentences have been done for you.

(Answers may vary.)

1 Picture a New England beach in autumn. The sky is clear, the

2 sun warms your face. The green sea has washed ashore almost 100 of

3 *its* ~~it's~~ most magnificent creatures whales to die. A biologist walks among

4 the bloating bodies of the whales and he is clearly puzzled.

5 Mass whale suicides, or "strandings" as they are called, occur year

6 after year. Many people have tried to understand these unusual

7 deaths, even Aristotle the ancient Greek, philosopher thought about the

8 whales deaths. Although he decided the whales may indeed be killing

9 themselves modern biologists are not so easily convinced."

10 One researcher points out that the whales may have once

11 been land dwelling animals. He thinks the whales may simply be

12 remembering their ancient roots, and beaching themselves to "go home."

13 This habit, however, would have put the whale close to extinction years

14 ago, so the idea doesn't make much sense.

15 A newer theory suggests that the whales blindly follow their food

16 supplies, into shallow water. For example, they may swim after a shoal

17 of squid, quickly eat their dinner, and then find themselves too close to

18 the shore.

46

19   Another theory says that whales follow the earths' magnetic forces

20 as though they were following a road map. The whales travel wherever

21 these forces lead. Unfortunately, the magnetic flow will sometimes cross

22 the shoreline and guide the whales along a collision course with the

23 beach.

24   Biologists realize, of course, that none of these findings are

25 complete explanations. Some feel that the strandings must have a

26 number of causes, not just one.

_____

_____

_____

_____

_____

_____

_____

_____

_____

Next Step In the space above, write freely for 3 to 5 minutes about punctuating writing. Consider what's easy or hard about it, what's important or confusing. Then, double-check your work by reviewing the punctuation rules and examples in *Write Source*.

Punctuation Review 2

(Answers may vary.)

1   Famous celebrities pose for pictures, sign autographs, and make a

2   lot of money. Going unnoticed, however, are the other stars—the animal

3   actors who work hard to keep these human celebrities in business. These

4   truly great stars are dogs like Timmy's Lassie and Marty Crane's Eddie

5   (on Frasier).

6   Lassie is probably the best-known television pet. However, the

7   dog we all now know as Lassie was not originally cast for the part.

8   He was hired instead as a stunt dog. Pal (Lassie's real name) was

9   a beautiful sable collie, and he was trained by Rudd Weatherwax, a

10 Hollywood dog trainer.

11   In one of the early filming sessions for the movie Lassie Come

12 Home, Lassie needed to swim across a raging river, pull herself out of

13 the water, and lie on the bank pretending to be dead. The starring dog

14 who originally played the part of Lassie could not be convinced to step

15 into the water. So Pal, the stunt dog, was called into action. Pal swam

16 across the raging river—even the swirling rapids—without any difficulty.

17 He didn't even shake out his coat when he got to the other side; he

18 lay down and pretended to be dead. The original starring dog was

19 fired‸ and Pal was hired as the new Lassie.

20   Eddie‸ the terrier who starred on the TV show <u>Frasier</u>‸ is also a

21 show‸stealing star. He is the talented dog who sometimes got more

22 laughs than the shows human star‸Kelsey Grammar. Eddie‸whose

23 real name is Moose‸did many comical tricks and made goofy facial

24 expressions that made it seem as though he knew just what would

25 make an audience laugh. He appeared on the covers of these popular

26 magazines‸<u>Life</u>‸<u>TV Guide</u>‸and <u>Entertainment Weekly</u>.

27   Animal actors are so well trained that we often forget that they

28 cant be taught to act in the same way that humans are taught.

29 Today‸with movies like <u>Air Bud</u> and <u>Bear</u>‸animal films are more

30 popular than ever. Thanks to the dedication of their trainers‸the work

31 of their agents‸and the talents of these incredible animals‸we are able

32 to enjoy a whole new generation of animal films and TV shows.

Capitalization 1

Good writers write good sentences. They also check their details and proofread their work to get rid of errors. In this exercise, you will proofread your writing for capitalization errors. The key to capitalizing correctly is remembering to capitalize all proper nouns and proper adjectives. (See 618.1–618.4, 620.5, and 622.2 in *Write Source* to review capitalization rules.)

Examples

Capitalize Historical Events and Proper Nouns:
The 2002 Winter Olympics were in Salt Lake City, Utah.

Capitalize Names and Words Used as Names:
Felix and Aunt Necia went to the games in Sydney, Australia.

Capitalize Titles Used with Names:
For years, President Juan A. Samaranch had been in charge of the games.

Capitalize Particular Sections of the Country:
The West Coast is the perfect place for skiing and sledding competitions.

> **Directions** Add capital letters to the following sentences as needed. The first sentence has been done for you.

1. The *I*nternational *O*lympic *C*ommittee decides where the games will be held.

2. Salt Lake *C*ity, *U*tah, was a perfect place for the winter games in 2002.

3. Winter conditions east of Salt *L*ake City are ideal for skiing and skating.

4. The *W*asatch *M*ountains are east of Salt *L*ake City.

5. During the planning for the games, *M*ayor *R*ocky *A*nderson met with the *U*nited *S*tates *O*lympic *C*ommittee.

6. A hare, a coyote, and a bear were the official *O*lympic mascots of the *S*alt *L*ake *C*ity games.

7. Their names were *S*wifter, *H*igher, and *S*tronger.

8. Officials from *S*alt *L*ake *C*ity hoped that many tourists would come to the games.

9. At our school, we studied the history of *U*tah.

10. *M*r. *M*arkus, our science teacher, visited *U*tah last spring.

11. The *O*lympic flame was first used in the opening ceremonies in the 1936 summer games in *B*erlin.

12. The *O*lympic flag has five rings that represent unity among the continents of *A*frica, the *A*mericas, *A*sia, *A*ustralia, and *E*urope.

13. My uncle was at the competition where Nadia *C*omaneci, a *R*omanian gymnast, earned the first perfect score in *O*lympic gymnastics.

14. The *I*nternational *S*ports *F*ederation decides the rules for gymnastic competitions.

15. World *W*ar I forced the cancellation of the 1916 games, planned for *B*erlin, *G*ermany.

16. At the 1936 *B*erlin games, *A*frican *A*merican athlete *J*esse *O*wens won gold medals in the 100-meter dash, 200-meter dash, and long jump event.

17. Last *F*riday, *M*ayor *J*ackson and five council members attended an Olympic site-selection meeting in *N*ew *Y*ork.

18. The meeting was sponsored by *M*cDonald's *C*orporation.

Next Step Using the Internet or other sources, research one of the past Olympic Games. Find out who the stars were and write about your findings in a paragraph or two. Share your writing aloud with a classmate. Then ask your classmate to check that you've capitalized words correctly.

Capitalization 2

Here's another exercise to help you to capitalize words correctly. Some helpful examples are given below. (See 624.1, 624.2, 626.1, and 626.2 in *Write Source* for more information and rules.

Examples

Capitalize the First Word at the Beginning of a Direct Quotation:

My friend Sasha said, "Well, my favorite Olympic sport is diving."

Capitalize Titles, Days, and Months:

The History of Olympic Games will be available in our library Friday, February 19.

Capitalize Organizations and Abbreviations:

The International Olympic Committee is sometimes referred to as the IOC.

> **Directions** Add capital letters where necessary to the following sentences. The first sentence has been done for you.

1. The ~~u.s.s.r.~~ *U.S.S.R.* sent its first *O*lympic team to the games in *H*elsinki, *F*inland.

2. The *E*ncyclopaedia *B*ritannica has a large section on the *O*lympic *G*ames.

3. My teacher said that the *R*ussians boycotted the games in *L*os *A*ngeles

   because *A*mericans boycotted the games in *M*oscow.

4. Felix said, "*T*he winter games were once held in *N*agano, *J*apan."

5. "I wish that I could have gone," he continued, "but it was too expensive."

6. "Well," I replied, "at least you got to watch the games on ~~tv~~ *TV*."

7. The ~~ioc~~ *IOC* has introduced some new sports to the *O*lympics in the last 10 years.

8. "*T*he number of women's sports has certainly increased," said Felicia.

9. *M*y uncle was a speed skater for the *D*utch team in the 2002 *O*lympics.

10. *T*he winter games were canceled in 1940 and 1944 because of *W*orld *W*ar II.

11. Chris Witty, a ~~u.s.~~ U.S. skater, won the 1000-meter speed-skating race in 2002.

12. Is *Blade Runner* a book about Olympic speed skating?

13. *Sports Illustrated* features many articles about the international stars of the Olympic Games.

14. After watching the 2002 Winter Olympic Games, my friend Ross said, "Those snowboarding events were awesome."

15. The IOC (International Olympic Committee) should not be confused with the ~~iac~~ IAC (International Athletic Conference) or the ~~ibc~~ IBC (International Bowling Congress).

16. Each country that participates in the Olympic Games has a National Olympic Committee (~~noc~~ NOC) that helps select athletes for its teams.

17. The official Web site of the ~~ioc~~ IOC is called the Olympic Movement, and it gives information about past, present, and future Olympic Games.

18. I remember my English teacher, Mr. Oden, saying, "My favorite sports poem is 'To an Athlete Dying Young' by A. E. Housman."

Next Step Write an imaginary conversation between you and your favorite Olympic or sports champion. Be sure to describe her or him first so that we will know more about the star. Share your writing aloud with a classmate. Then ask her or him to correct any capitalization errors.

Abbreviations and Numbers

Using abbreviations is convenient, but if you overuse them or use them incorrectly, they can make your writing confusing.

Using numbers can be a bit tricky. The big question is whether you should write numbers out or use figures. The type of writing often determines your choice. In technical and business writing, figures are often used. In general writing, however, numbers are more often spelled out. (For more information about numbers and abbreviations, see pages 634, 636, 638, and 640 in *Write Source*.)

Examples

Abbreviations:

Mr. **and** Mrs. **James Wilkins,** Jr. **are returning from their trip to Ethiopia.**
(Acceptable)

They came home to the U.S. **on** Thurs., **but they will return to Africa in** Dec.
(Unacceptable: Do not abbreviate the names of states, countries, days, or months in formal writing.)

Numerals Only:

Please read pages 345–362 **in chapter** 3 **for tomorrow.**

Numerals in Compound Modifiers:

I asked for three 13-year-old **volunteers.**

 Directions   Correct any abbreviation or number error by drawing a line through the error and writing the correct form above it. Do not change any abbreviation or number that is used correctly. The first sentence has been done for you.

Twelve
1. ~~12~~ of Hugo's best friends came to visit him.

2. On May ~~six~~ *6*, Hugo and his friends celebrated his 10th birthday.

3. Last year, when Hugo turned nine, his parents bought him a new bike.

4. His father is a ~~prof.~~ *professor* who works for ~~nasa.~~ *NASA*

5. His mother is an ~~m.d.~~ *M.D.* who specializes in ~~ER~~ *emergency room* medicine.

6. Now that he is going to be ~~ten,~~ *10* Hugo is hoping to get ~~3~~ *three* presents for his birthday.

7. Someday Hugo would like to work for the ~~cia~~ *CIA* or ~~fbi,~~ *FBI* so he wants a spy kit.

8. He would also like ~~2~~ *two* 250-piece sets of building blocks.

9. The gift he really hopes to receive is an IBM ~~pc.~~ *PC*

10. Hugo might have to wait another year for his ~~pc.~~ *PC*

11. His pal Joey gave Hugo a geode from ~~Tenn.,~~ *Tennessee* and his friend Jason gave him a wooden box from ~~Ark.~~ *Arkansas*

12. But the strangest gift Hugo received came from his dad's friend Gregory Burns, ~~PHD,~~ *Ph.D.* a ~~N.A.S.A.~~ *NASA* rocket scientist.

13. Dr. Burns gave Hugo a ~~twelve~~-*12*-ounce moon rock brought back on *Apollo 17*, which landed on the moon ~~Dec.~~ *December* 11, 1972.

14. Joey hung around, and he and Hugo watched ~~W.W.F.~~ *WWF* wrestling on the WB network and saw about 1 million commercials.

15. Joey's dad picked him up and drove down Highway ~~thirty-six~~ *36* back to their home.

16. Hugo had a great birthday, but his mom and dad were exhausted from having to deal with ~~13~~ *thirteen* 10-year-old boys from 10:30 ~~AM~~ *a.m. (or) A.M.* to 7:00 ~~PM.~~ *p.m. (or) P.M.*

Next Step Write a paragraph about the best birthday present you ever received. Share the paragraph with your classmates and have them check for correct use of abbreviations and numbers.

Capitalization and Abbreviations Review

Attention to detail means different things to different people. To a writer it means carefully reviewing a final draft to make sure that every *i* is dotted, every *t* is crossed, and every capital letter is in place. (See pages 618–626, 634, and 636 in *Write Source* for more information on capitalization and abbreviations.)

> **Directions** Cross out any word or letter below that is capitalized or abbreviated incorrectly. Correct each error and add punctuation where needed.

1. home of mrs. goodwrench *[M G]*

2. The Mayor is going to speak Tues. *[m] [Tuesday.]*

3. Did you call me, uncle Jim? *[U]*

4. Go East until you come to the library. *[e]*

5. Isn't your Mother from the East? *[m]*

6. This humid august weather is unbearable. *[A]*

7. I heard mom calling for you, Dad. *[M]*

8. I've always liked History Courses. Are you taking history 201 next Fall? *[h] [c] [H] [f]*

9. Mr. Kipp let me read there's a bat in bunk five. *[T] [B] [B] [F]*

10. Castles were quite common in the Middle ages. *[A]*

11. Are you going to take that job out west? *[W]*

12. No, I am going to take the job down South.

13. the Battle of Bunker Hill

14. She shouted, "don't touch the stove!" *[D]*

15. Navajo pottery, Dutch pastry, Chinese muslin

16. Have you read "by the waters of babylon"? *[B W] [B]*

17. The Chicago Trib. is a fine daily newspaper. *[Tribune]*

18. George W. Bush was once the governor of TX. *[Texas]*

19. "make room," barked the mover. "This piano is heavy." *[M]*

20. J C R
"jerome," yelled coach rogers, "stay

back on defense!"

21. P
They'll put people on the Planet

Mars.

22. lakes Michigan and Superior

23. R
Colorado river

24. T B M S S
the bailey middle school science
C
club will sell refreshments.

25. M.D.
Bob Madsen, m.d.

26. M
Mr. Jackson, mark's father, joined
H
the staff at Trinity hospital.

27. C
Kellogg's crispix cereal

28. F A
the first amendment to the
C United States of America
constitution of the U S A

29. He's busy with his American

History 212 assignment.

30. O
Hawaii is in the Pacific ocean.

Directions Supply the necessary capital letters in the following narrative. (There are 49 capital letters needed.)

1   A
america's best-loved radio program, A P H C
a prairie home companion, left the

2   J B
air on june 13, 1987, at the height of its popularity. broadcast from the

3   W T S P M
world theater in st. paul, minnesota, the show charmed millions of listeners.

4   H G K
host garrison keillor took his audience into the heart and soul of an

5   M L W
imaginary town in minnesota called lake wobegon—also known by the

6   T T T T F D C N
following title: "the town that time forgot and the decades could not

7   I W F E O L P
improve." who could ever forget father emil, our lady of perpetual

8   R S T B K B P
responsibility, the sidetrack tap, bertha's kitty boutique, powdermilk

9   B R P G G T S U
biscuits, ralph's pretty good grocery, and "the statue of the unknown

10 N
norwegian"? After several years, the show returned to the airwaves due to

11 popular demand.

Capitalization Mixed Review

Directions Carefully read the following essay and add capital letters wherever necessary. (For capitalization rules, see pages 618–626 in *Write Source*.)

1   Baseball legends like babe [B] ruth [R], hank [H] aaron [A], and roger [R] maris [M] have

2   helped make baseball an all-american [A] pastime. for [F] years fans crowded

3   into stadiums around the country to witness these home-run hitters at

4   their best.

5   one [O] of the most gifted and popular players of all time was babe [B] ruth [R].

6   babe's [B] real name was george [G] herman [H] ruth [R], and he was born in baltimore [B],

7   maryland [M]. babe [B] ruth [R] pitched for the boston [B] red [R] sox [S], played outfield for the

8   new [N] york [Y] yankees [Y], and even coached for the brooklyn [B] dodgers [D]. though [T] ruth [R]

9   was very talented in all these areas, the thing he is most remembered

10   for is his home-run hitting. his [H] record of 60 home runs in one season was

11   unchallenged until 1962 when roger [R] maris [M], another american [A] league [L] player,

12   broke the record with 61 home runs in one season. babe [B] ruth [R] was elected to

13   the baseball [B] hall [H] of fame [F] in 1936.

14   At the time of maris' [M] accomplishment, ford [F] c. [C] frick [F], the baseball

15   commissioner, declared that maris [M] had not broken ruth's [R] record. frick [F] felt

16   that because maris [M] had 162 games in the season and ruth [R] only had 154

17   games, maris [M] did not break the record. it [I] was not until 1991 that maris' [M]

18   record was acknowledged without dispute. maris [M] retired from baseball in

19   1968 with a career total of 275 home runs.

20   *H**A*
   hank aaron, who played during 23 seasons in the major leagues, broke

21   *B**R**I**A**B*
   another record set by babe ruth. in 1954, aaron joined the braves, who at

22   *B**B**B**A**G*
   the time, played in boston. by the time the braves moved to atlanta, georgia,

23   *A**A**A*
   in 1965, aaron had hit 398 home runs. On april 8, 1974, aaron hit his 715th

24   *B**R**A*
   home run, breaking a record held by babe ruth since 1935. aaron was

25   *B**H**F*
   elected to the baseball hall of fame in 1982.

26   *A*
   as fans pour into stadiums around the country, they hope to see a

27   *B**R**R**M**H**A**T*
   player as great as babe ruth, roger maris, or hank aaron. the outstanding

28   *A*
   players and their home-run records make baseball one of america's

29 favorite sports!

Spelling and Plurals

Developing spelling skills takes time and patience. Using your spell checker and a dictionary can help. (See pages 630, 632, and 642 in *Write Source* to review rules about spelling correctly. Also use the guide on pages 645–651.)

Directions Complete the following sentences by writing the correctly spelled word in parentheses on the line provided. The first sentence has been done for you.

1. At _____*rodeos*_____, cowboys show their skills at _____*handling*_____ cattle.
   (rodeos, rodeoes)   (handleing, handling)

2. At these competitions, _____*riding*_____ skills are important.
   (rideing, riding)

3. Steer _____*wrestling*_____ is a popular event for competitors.
   (wrestleing, wrestling)

4. _____*Bulldogging*_____ is another name for this event.
   (Bulldogging, Bulldoging)

5. In this event, the cowboy tries _____*grabbing*_____ the horns of the steer
   (grabbing, grabing)

   to twist the head of the animal to one side.

6. The steer loses its balance, _____*forcing*_____ it to fall to the ground.
   (forcing, forceing)

7. Calf _____*roping*_____ is another important skill for ranchers and cowboys.
   (ropeing, roping)

8. The cowboy _____*lassoes*_____ the calf with a _____*looped*_____ rope.
   (lassoes, lassos)   (looped, loopped)

9. The cowboy then _____*ties*_____ together three of the calf's _____*feet*_____.
   (ties, tys)   (feet, feets)

10. In barrel _____racing_____, competitors ride horses around barrels.
(*racing, raceing*)

11. Some may _____believe_____ rodeos are dangerous for the animals.
(*believe, beleive*)

12. However, people are _____careful_____ not to hurt the animals.
(*careful, carful*)

13. While _____battling_____ these animals, the cowboys are practicing
(*battleing, battling*)

skills that will help them in _____raising_____ their livestock.
(*raiseing, raising*)

14. My family and _____friends_____ are _____committed_____ to helping
(*freinds, friends*)   (*committed, commited*)

_____children_____ understand the sport.
(*children, childrens*)

15. In junior rodeos, kids rope goats instead of _____calves_____, but
(*calves, calfs*)

_____neither_____ of those animals is easy to rope.
(*niether, neither*)

16. Rodeo clowns throw _____handfuls_____ of confetti to distract angry bulls.
(*handfuls, handsful*)

17. At the _____beginning_____ of their act, some clowns play _____banjos_____.
(*beginning, begining*)   (*banjoes, banjos*)

18. Rodeo cowboys compete by riding _____steers_____, bulls, and broncos.
(*steers, steeres*)

19. Professional rodeo cowboys buy _____their_____ hats and boots at the many
(*their, thier*)

Cowboy Country Stores located in the western United States.

Next Step Write a paragraph about an interesting sports event. Edit your paragraph for correct spelling. Share the paragraph with a classmate. Ask the classmate to check your writing for correct spelling and use of plurals.

Using the Right Word 1

It's important to use the right word whenever you are going to share your thoughts in a formal or semi-formal situation. Whenever you have a usage question, refer to "Using the Right Word," pages 652–658 in *Write Source*.

Examples

It's nice to have a lot of friends.

The charity accepts any kind of donation.
All my books except one are covered.

Banks have a large amount of money.
A number of people waited for tickets.

One small tree grew among the flowers.
Nothing comes between those two friends.

I'll bring my comics to your house.
Take these books to the library.

These fries are altogether too salty.
We were all together at the playground.

Dwight already brushed his teeth.
My room is all ready for fresh paint.

Mom brakes for animals in the road.
Did your ball break my window?

Stand beside me for this picture.
Besides soccer, Drew plays tennis.

The base of this lamp is quite heavy.
Regina plays the bass trombone.

 Directions   If the underlined word is incorrect, cross out the word and write the correct form above it. Do not change a word that is correct. The first sentence has been done for you.

1   On a hot summer morning in 1939, the people who lived in tiny Orange

     all ready
2   City, Iowa, were ~~already~~ for the Fourth of July celebration. In the village

            between
3   park, a large cannon lay on a frame ~~among~~ two wooden-spoked wheels.

 Beside   *base*
4   ~~Besides~~ the big gun, three huge balls rested on a square wooden ~~bass~~. Two

5   uniformed World War I veterans stood on either side of the cannon. A large

 number
6   ~~amount~~ of spectators had gathered around them.

7   The mayor was just finishing his speech: " . . . and the reason we're

all together
8   ~~altogether~~ in this safe, free, grand country of ours is not simply a result

a lot
9   of this being our place of birth. As ~~alot~~ of you older folks remember, when

accepted
10   President Wilson told us to take up arms, we all willingly ~~excepted~~ that

11   command. When the call to duty came, we believed that free people cannot

break
12   remain free when others are trying to ~~brake~~ up their democracy!"

13   The mayor stabbed his large right hand into the air to emphasize

took   *except*
14   his last point: "So our soldier boys ~~brought~~ nothing ~~accept~~ their guns and

bring
15   bullets over to the other side of the ocean, so they could ~~take~~ back a new

16   lease on freedom to this side of the ocean!"

a lot   *besides*
17   There were ~~alot~~ of children among the crowd, ~~beside~~ the usual farmers,

altogether
18   housewives, and a number of storekeepers. They were ~~all together~~ energized.

all together
19   And now, ~~altogether~~, they cheered the mayor and the round-shouldered

already
20   veteran who had ~~all ready~~ lit the fuse on the huge, old cannon.

Next Step Write a short incident report about a recent event that surprised (or frustrated) you. Use five or more of the words you just learned about in this lesson. Circle them. (See pages 150–151 in *Write Source* for writing guidelines and a sample incident report.)

Using the Right Word 2

For examples and explanations, see pages 660–666 in *Write Source*.

Examples

I hope I never see a real prison cell.
Tamika will sell candy at the game.

A spicy sauce complements the potatoes.
Ms. Rau compliments students on their work.

The tree creaks when the wind blows.
D. J. likes to go fishing in the creek.

This pet store has fewer birds than that one.
Dad has less hair now than when he was 20.

Hunter is such a good dog.
Nadine acted well in the school play.

We heard the bell ringing miles away.
A herd of mountain goats crossed the road.

 Directions If the underlined word is incorrect, cross out the word and write the correct form above it. Do not change a word that is correct. The first sentence has been done for you.

1. Monique ~~herd~~ *heard* a ~~creek~~ *creak* every time she stepped on a certain spot on the floor.

2. The longer you stay in bed after sunrise, the ~~less~~ *fewer* things you'll accomplish that day.

3. You'll get along ~~good~~ *well* with others if you give compliments when they are deserved.

4. Have you even seen a herd of cattle grazing near a ~~creak~~ *creek* in a farm field?

5. I might try to ~~cell~~ *sell* my stamp collection.

6. Wow, Rita, that shade of blue really ~~compliments~~ *complements* your hair and skin.

7. This is a ~~well~~ *good* plant for desert climates since it requires ~~fewer~~ *less* water than most others.

8. The ~~sell~~ *cell* of a honeycomb has six sides.

9. I ~~herd~~ *heard* a little ~~creek~~ *creak* from the cricket out on our back porch.

Using the Right Word 3

For examples and explanations, see pages 668–676 in *Write Source*.

Examples

A contractor will lay the carpet tomorrow.
Rudy will lie in the hammock for hours.

I need two lead pencils for the test.
Seiko led the horse to the barn.

John Lennon said, "Give peace a chance."
Cut me a piece of that pie.

It looks like it's going to storm.
This book is missing some of its pages.

Don't leave the milk on the counter.
Mom will not let me pierce my navel.

My principal goal is to go to college.
I follow the principle of "honesty always."

 Directions Correct any errors by drawing a line through the word and writing the correct form above it. Do not change any word that is correct. The first sentence has been done for you.

1. Based on the ~~principals~~ *principles* of science, I have been ~~lead~~ *led* to believe that clean

   energy is in our future.

2. If LaTanya and Jawann would just ~~let~~ *leave* each other alone, there would be

   ~~piece~~ *peace* in the house!

3. ~~Its~~ *It's* rare for my cat to ~~lay~~ *lie* anywhere except the windowsill on a sunny day.

4. "I can see that lead statue is heavy," said Scott. "Please ~~leave~~ *let* me carry it."

5. He said, "Go ahead and ~~lie~~ *lay* it right here on the floor for a minute."

6. The ~~principle~~ *principal* reason Corentine's chameleon lost a ~~peace~~ *piece* of ~~it's~~ *its* tail was that

   someone had stepped on it.

7. There are two ~~principals~~ *principles* that I try to live out—being dependable and

   respectful.

Using the Right Word 4

Here are some words that can be found on pages 678–682 in *Write Source*.

Examples

I don't think this is the right address.
Corey will write some instructions.

Riding a stationary bike is good exercise.
Aunt Ginny has personalized stationery.

Decorative stitching lines the seams.
It doesn't seem like it's really spring.

Derek likes vanilla more than chocolate.
Read the book first; then see the movie.

Sakura threw the spoiled food away.
We went in through the exit door.

Should we wait for Jordan?
A gallon's weight is about eight pounds.

> **Directions** Correct any errors by drawing a line through the word and writing the correct form above it. Do not change any word that is correct.

1. Do members of your family often ~~right~~ *write* letters?

2. Do you enjoy communicating ~~threw~~ *through* the mail?

3. Do you look like a ~~stationery~~ *stationary* statue as you wait for the postal carrier?

4. Some people write such long letters that they exceed the postal ~~wait~~ *weight* limits.

5. If a letter ~~seams~~ *seems* heavier ~~then~~ *than* one ounce, check its weight.

6. If that happens to you, try using lighter ~~stationary~~ *stationery*; then just one stamp will be the ~~write~~ *right* postage.

7. As, I ~~through~~ *threw* a letter in a mailbox, the ~~seem~~ *seam* of my sleeve got caught on the edge of the box.

8. After I ~~right~~ *write* a letter, ~~than~~ *then* I can hardly ~~weight~~ *wait* to get a reply.

Using the Right Word Review

Directions Correct any errors by drawing a line through the word and writing the correct form above it. Do not change any word that is correct.

1. Last week, we counted 13 hawks ~~altogether~~ *all together*, but that was ~~less then~~ *fewer than* we counted the week before.

2. The ~~principle~~ *principal* of our school often gives ~~complements~~ *compliments* to students.

3. Right after Sanjeet said he wouldn't ~~brake~~ *break* the dish, he was picking up its ~~peaces~~ *pieces* and trying to glue it back together.

4. ~~Its~~ *It's* not true, but it ~~seams~~ *seems* as though we breezed ~~threw~~ *through* sixth grade in just a few months.

5. ~~Alot~~ *A lot* of people would be happy to ~~except~~ *accept* the Nobel ~~Piece~~ *Peace* Prize.

6. The ~~creek~~ *creak* of the rocking chair could be ~~herd~~ *heard* throughout the house.

7. I can't ~~weight~~ *wait* to see this movie; ~~it's~~ *its* reviews are very ~~well~~ *good*.

8. Although the time ~~seams write~~ *seems right* to sell the car, he's not sure he'll get the ~~number~~ *amount* of money he wants for it.

9. Clyde ~~lead~~ *led* the two boys to a creek where the ~~base~~ *bass* swam freely.

10. The dog behaves ~~good~~ *well* on the leash when I ~~bring~~ *take* her out for a walk.

11. Satinka told her mom, "Drive up ~~besides~~ *beside* the curb and step on the ~~break~~ *brake*."

12. I don't know of anyone ~~accept~~ *except* me who can ~~lay~~ *lie* down, take a short nap, ~~than~~ *then* be refreshed and wide awake.

13. Grandma takes pride in picking the right ~~peace~~ *piece* of meat from ~~between~~ *among* all of those in the butcher case.

14. The base of our ~~stationery~~ *stationary* bike takes up ~~fewer~~ *less* space ~~then~~ *than* our trampoline.

Sentence and Paragraph Activities

The activities in this section cover three important areas: (1) the basic parts of sentences and paragraphs, (2) common sentence errors, and (3) ways to add variety to sentences. Most activities include a main practice part in which you review, combine, or analyze different sentences. In addition, the **Next Step** activities give you follow-up practice with certain skills.

Subjects and Predicates 1

Careful writers write clear and complete sentences. A sentence consists of two parts: the subject and the predicate. The **subject** is the part that is doing something or about which something is being said. The **predicate** is the part that says something about the subject. In a sentence, the subject and predicate fit together to form a complete thought. (See 690.2, 692.2, and 694.1 in *Write Source* to examine subjects and predicates in more detail.)

Examples

Simple Subject:
Marjorie **owns a robot that carries her books for her.**
(The simple subject is who or what the sentence is about.)

Simple Predicate:
Felicia's robot will obey **all her commands.**
(The predicate—or verb—tells something about the subject. *Remember:* helping verbs like "will" are often part of the simple predicate.)

Understood Subject:
Think about what a robot could do in your home. (understood subject: You**)**
(When the sentence is a command or a request, the subject is usually not stated. The person to whom the command is directed—"You"—is the subject of the sentence.)

 Directions In the following sentences, underline the simple subject once and the simple predicate twice. The first sentence has been done for you.

1. Robots work in homes, businesses, and schools.

2. In medical laboratories, robots handle hazardous materials.

3. At the General Motors Corporation, robots work on assembly lines

   performing tasks like welding and painting.

4. Most boring or dangerous tasks are done by GMC's robots.

5. Other companies use specially designed robots for tasks that require

   precision.

6. Robots explore sunken ships, distant planets, and active volcanoes.

7. Miguel's toy soldier is really a small robot.

8. Think of all the robot-like toys you own. (*You*)

9. Jeremiah dreams of owning his own robot someday.

10. Elena wishes for a robot to do her math homework for her.

11. I want robots for mowing my lawn, delivering my newspapers, and cleaning

    my room.

12. Maybe my teacher will be replaced by a computerized robot.

13. Imagine what the world would be like with thousands of robots. (*You*)

14. One of the stars of *The Red Planet* was Robby the Robot.

15. Have you ever seen a robot at work?

16. Our family's robot could get me a glass of milk.

17. Most robots in films and TV shows are not very realistic.

18. Can you name your favorite robot?

Next Step Imagine having your own robot. Write a paragraph describing what your personal robot would be like. Then draw an illustration to accompany your paragraph. Share the illustration and the paragraph with a classmate. Have your classmate check your writing for complete sentences.

Subjects and Predicates 2

There are simple subjects and simple predicates. But what about all those other words in the sentence? The words that describe the subject or predicate are called *modifiers.* Modifiers change or add to the meaning of the subject or predicate. Together, the simple subject plus its modifiers make the **complete subject,** and the simple predicate plus its modifiers make the **complete predicate.** (See 690.3 and 692.3 in *Write Source* for more information.)

Examples

Complete Subject:

The large, umbrella-shaped parachute **saved the life of the inexperienced pilot**.

(The complete subject is the simple subject—"parachute"—plus all its modifiers.)

Complete Predicate:

The large, umbrella-shaped parachute saved the life of the inexperienced pilot.

(The complete predicate is the simple predicate—"saved"—plus all its modifiers.)

 Directions In the following sentences, divide the complete subject and the complete predicate with a slash (/). Then, underline the simple subject once and the simple predicate twice. The first sentence has been done for you.

1. French aeronaut <u>Jean Pierre Blanchard</u>/<u><u>dropped</u></u> a dog in the first parachute "jump" in 1785.

2. <u>Blanchard</u>/successfully <u><u>made</u></u> the first human parachute drop in 1793.

3. <u>Parachutes</u>/are now <u><u>required</u></u> for all balloonists and pilots.

4. The large silk or nylon parachute <u>canopy</u>/<u><u>has</u></u> a small vent hole in its center that expands to lessen the shock when the parachute opens.

5. The 24-foot, multipaneled <u>parachute</u>/<u>is pulled</u> from the jumper's backpack by a smaller parachute.

6. <u>Parachutes</u>/<u>have been used</u> during wars to drop troops, tanks, and equipment behind enemy lines.

7. Sport <u>parachuting</u>, also known as skydiving,/<u>became</u> popular in the 1970s.

8. Steerable <u>parachutes</u> that allow safer landings/<u>have made</u> the sport even more popular today.

9. <u>Parachutists</u>/<u>compete</u> in skydiving competitions by doing a series of acrobatic maneuvers before reaching parachute-opening altitude.

10. <u>Teams</u> of free-falling skydivers/<u>compete</u> by forming as many geometric patterns as possible before opening their chutes.

11. <u>(You)</u>/<u>Consider</u> the risk of skydiving before taking the plunge.

12. Steerable <u>parachutes</u>/<u>are</u> quite different from hang gliders.

13. In 1972, a Yugoslavian flight <u>attendant</u>/<u>survived</u> a fall from 33,370 feet without a parachute.

14. The <u>record</u> for the longest fall with a parachute/<u>is</u> 40 minutes.

Next Step Skydiving is a sport that requires skill and daring. Write a paragraph explaining why you would or would not want to be a skydiver. Share the paragraph with a classmate. Be sure to write in complete sentences.

Compound Subjects and Predicates

Combining short, related sentences into longer sentences is valuable practice for improving your writing style. Writers can combine short sentences using coordinating conjunctions. This can result in a sentence with either a **compound subject** (two or more simple subjects) or a **compound predicate** (two or more simple predicates) or both. (For more information about compound subjects and compound predicates, see 690.4 and 692.6 in *Write Source*.)

Examples

Compound Subject:
Golf and writing are just two of Jack Nicklaus' talents.

Compound Predicate:
Jack Nicklaus went to Ohio State University and played in the Professional Golf Association.

Compound Subject and Compound Predicate:
Jack and Ken Bowden co-wrote books and published their work.

 Directions In the following sentences, underline the subject with one line and the predicate with two lines. Remember that some sentences have only a compound subject, some have only a compound predicate, and some have both. The first one has been done for you.

1. Jack Nicklaus won the U. S. Amateur championship and set a record for an amateur in the U. S. Open in 1961.

2. Keenan and Angelica watched a movie about Nicklaus and wished they could see him in person.

3. Jack and golf course architect Pete Dye worked together to design several gold courses.

4. Jack Nicklaus was named PGA Player of the Year five times and was elected to the World Golf Hall of Fame.

5. Jack and his wife had five children.

6. Nicklaus designed Muirfield Village Golf Course and wrote several books.

7. *Golf My Way, Nicklaus by Design,* and *The Full Swing* are just a few of the books written by Jack Nicklaus.

8. Nicklaus founded and owns Nicklaus Golf Equipment.

9. Nicklaus, his four sons, and his son-in-law have a partnership for designing and building golf courses.

10. Nicklaus and fellow golfer Annika Sorenstam helped to bring golf to the Olympics in 2016 and 2020.

Next Step Using the Internet or other sources, research a sports or entertainment figure. Write a paragraph or two about your findings using some compound subjects and compound predicates. Share your writing with a classmate and ask him or her to check for complete sentences and proper use of compound subjects and predicates.

Clauses

Clauses, like phrases, are word groups that add information to a sentence. Unlike phrases, clauses always have a subject and a predicate. Clauses that form a complete thought are called **independent clauses,** and clauses that do not form a complete thought are called **dependent** or **subordinate clauses.** (*Write Source* gives more information about clauses on page 698.)

Examples

Dependent Clause:
Even though she was at the peak of her career,
Susan Colby retired from running in 2002.

Independent Clause:
Susan Colby retired from running in 2002 **even though she was at the peak of her career.**

Susan Colby was a fantastic runner**, and** she won many medals.
(Two independent clauses are separated by a comma and a coordinating conjunction or by a semicolon.)

 Directions In each of the following sentences, identify the italicized clause. Write "I" for independent or "D" for dependent. The first sentence has been done for you.

_____*I*_____ **1.** Though she grew up in a poor area of her town,

   Susan Colby worked hard to overcome poverty.

_____*I*_____ **2.** *Susan was a gymnast at a young age,* but she ended up being a

   track star.

_____*D*_____ **3.** *After she won her fifteenth race in 2001,* Colby retired from her

   running career.

_____*I*_____ **4.** Colby's daughter, Lindsay, was also a runner, and *she competed*

   throughout high school and college.

_____I_____ **5.** *Susan Colby coached high school track,* and her team won the state championship two years in a row.

_____D_____ **6.** What do you think motivated Susan *when she ran?*

_____I_____ **7.** After she retired from running, *Susan wanted to write a book about her life.*

_____D_____ **8.** *Although she officially retired from competition in 2001,* Colby continued to coach track for many years.

_____D_____ **9.** *Due to her incredible career,* many people were inspired by Susan Colby.

Next Step Do some research using the Internet or another source to find information about another athlete. Write five sentences using dependent and independent clauses. Share your writing aloud with a classmate and then check each other's work for correct use of clauses.

Adverb Clauses

An **adverb clause** is a clause that modifies a verb, and adjective, or an adverb. Adverb clauses tell when, where, why, how, or to what extent. (For more information, see page 698 in *Write Source*.)

Examples

Answers where:
Wherever we went, **we stayed with relatives**.

Answers when:
Juan gave the correct answer, after pausing to think.

Answers how much:
I took all my coins **to the bank**.

Answers why:
Because it was a beautiful day, **we went for a picnic**.

 Directions In each of the following sentences, underline the adverb clause. The first sentence has been done for you.

1. Ray and I decided to see a movie <u>after we had dinner</u>.

2. <u>Since I don't like scary movies</u>, we went to a comedy.

3. We bought popcorn and drinks <u>before the movie started</u>.

4. Ray chose two seats for us <u>where he could find them</u>.

5. Suddenly the lights came on in the theater <u>because the film broke</u>.

6. <u>While the projectionist fixed the film</u>, we sat and waited.

7. I enjoyed the movie <u>more than Ray did</u>.

8. Later, I returned to my seat <u>so that I could retrieve my hat</u>.

9. Ray's mom was parked <u>down the street</u>.

10. She drove me home <u>to my house</u>.

11. <u>When I walked in</u>, my dad was watching TV.

Next Step Write five sentences about an experience you have had. Try to include an adverb clause in every sentence. Exchange your sentences with a partner. Underline each clause in your partner's sentences and draw an arrow to the word it modifies. Then discuss each other's work.

Adjective Clauses

An **adjective clause** is a subordinate clause that describes or modifies a noun or pronoun by telling what kind, how many, or which one. Adjective clauses are always introduced by a relative pronoun—*who, whom, which, whose,* or *that.* (For more information, see page 698 in *Write Source*.)

Examples

Answers what kind:
A bicycle that has wide tires is good for riding on dirt trails.

Answers how many:
The team that won three games took home the trophy.

Answers which one:
The tennis player who wore the red shirt won the match.

 Directions In each of the following sentences, underline the adjective clause and circle the noun or pronoun it modifies. The first sentence has been done for you.

1. My brother and I went to the (library) that featured my favorite author.

2. The (author,) who writes mysteries, is quite well-known.

3. The library is on (Main Street,) which is a fifteen minute walk from our house.

4. We arrived early and went to the (section) that contains mystery books.

5. I couldn't find the book I was looking for and asked the (librarian,) who is friendly and helpful, for assistance.

6. The author spoke in the large (room) that is on the second floor.

7. He read a chapter from his next (novel,) which is coming out next month.

8. He signed (books) that people brought with them when he finished reading.

9. The author signed my (book,) which I bought at the book store.

10. He signed it with a (pen) that was made of silver.

11. My (brother,) who doesn't read mysteries, enjoyed the event as much as I did.

Next Step Write a paragraph of at least five sentences that describes a concert, play, or movie you attended. Include one adjective phrase in each sentence. Read your work aloud to the class.

Phrases

A phrase is a group of words that lacks a subject, a predicate, or both. In many cases, a phrase works as a modifier (describes something) in a sentence. Most phrases are named for the function they serve in a sentence (noun phrase, adverb phrase, verb phrase). Study the examples below and the ones on page 700 in *Write Source*.

. . . and a large order of phrases

Examples

Noun Phrase: **Our summer trip** (This phrase acts as a noun.)

Prepositional Phrase: **to Florida** (This phrase modifies the subject "trip.")

Verb Phrase: **was spent** (This phrase acts as a verb.)

Adverb Phrase: **very excitedly** (This phrase modifies the verb "was spent.")

Verbal Phrase: **viewing the many sights** (This phrase modifies "was spent.")

 Directions Identify the underlined phrase in each sentence below. The first sentence has been done for you.

_____*adverb phrase*_____ 1. <u>Early this morning</u>, the Phillips family left for the airport.

___*prepositional phrase*___ 2. They waited at the busy airport to catch their flight <u>to Orlando, Florida</u>.

_____*adverb phrase*_____ 3. During their wait, they talked <u>very excitedly</u> about visiting the special attractions at the amusement park.

_____*verb phrase*_____ 4. Mikah <u>was going</u> to see all the exhibits, which feature the cultures of 11 different countries.

_____*noun phrase*_____ 5. People of every age enjoy <u>this exciting and educational experience</u>.

verbal phrase   **6.** <u>Having a tight budget</u>, Mikah and Ruby's parents were determined not to spend too much money.

prepositional phrase   **7.** With a tour package, they were able to save money <u>on entrance passes</u> to the amusement park.

verb phrase   **8.** Ruby <u>has been dreaming</u> about this vacation for years.

noun phrase   **9.** <u>The Phillips's vacation</u> lasted for five days.

Directions Write 5 sentences below about a trip you took (or would like to take). Use a different type of phrase in each sentence. Underline the phrases. When you are finished, share your sentences aloud with a partner.

1. _____

_____

_____

2. _____

_____

3. _____

_____

4. _____

_____

5. _____

_____

Adverb Phrases

An **adverb phrase** is a group of words that describes a verb or adverb. Adverb phrases tell where, when, or in what way. (For more information, look at page 700 in *Write Source*.)

Examples

Telling when:
We arrived at the party in the early evening.

Telling in what way and where:
With a gleam in his eye, **the batter swung** at the ball.

Telling for what purpose:
Phil brought the apple to school for his teacher.

 Directions Identify each adverb phrase in the following sentences. Underline the phrase and draw an arrow pointing to the word or words that it modifies. Some sentences have more than one adverb phrase. The first sentence has been done for you.

1. Jorge and Dan left the house <u>at the first sign of dawn.</u>

2. They rode their bikes <u>over the hill</u> and <u>down to the lake.</u>

3. It began to rain <u>when Jorge looked</u> <u>over the smooth water.</u>

4. <u>With a glum expression,</u> the two boys got out their fishing poles.

5. The fish started biting, much <u>to the boys' surprise.</u>

6. They fished all afternoon <u>until five o'clock</u>.

7. The boys brought the fish they caught home <u>for Dan's mother</u>.

8. She cooked the fish <u>in a frying pan</u>.

9. They ate the fish <u>until their stomachs were full</u>.

10. Then, <u>with a keen intensity</u>, the boys played video games.

11. Jorge went home <u>before ten o'clock</u>.

Next Step Write six sentences about a fun activity you did with a friend. Include an adverb phrase in each sentence. Share your sentences with a partner and explain which verb or adverb is modified by each adverb phrase.

Adjective Phrases

An **adjective phrase** is a group of words that acts as an adjective in a sentence, modifying a noun or pronoun. An adjective phrase tells what kind, how many, or which one. (For more information, see page 700 in *Write Source*.)

Examples

Tells which one:
He wore the jacket with the blue stripes.

Tells what kind:
Paulo received an invitation to the surprise party.

Tells how many:
The tops of four mountains **were visible on the horizon.**

 Directions Rewrite each sentence below, changing the underlined adjective or noun into an adjective phrase.

Example: The artist's signature *appeared on the painting.*
The signature of the artist appeared on the painting.

1. My dad brought home a spotted dog as our new pet.

    My dad brought home a dog with spots as our new pet.

    _____

2. I feed him canned food twice a day.

    I feed him food from a can twice a day.

    _____

3. I buy our dog food at the corner pet store.

    I buy our dog food at the pet store on the corner.

    _____

4. Every day I take him <u>neighborhood</u> walking.

Every day I take him walking in the neighborhood.

5. I use a <u>leather</u> leash when I walk him.

I use a leash made of leather when I walk him.

6. When we return, he likes to curl up on the <u>back</u> patio.

When we return, he likes to curl up on the patio in the back.

7. My dog will go to sleep on our <u>yellow-striped</u> couch.

My dog will go to sleep on our couch with yellow stripes.

8. His favorite spot to sleep, however, is my <u>bed</u> pillow.

His favorite spot to sleep, however, is the pillow on my bed.

Next Step Write a paragraph about your favorite pet or animal. Include at least one adjective phrase in each sentence. Read your paragraph to a partner and ask him or her to identify each adjective phrase. Then do the same after your partner reads his or her paragraph to you.

Appositive Phrases

An **appositive phrase** is a group of words that rename a noun or pronoun it follows. An appositive phrase adds new information about the noun or pronoun. (For more information, see page 512 in *Write Source*.)

Examples

The cat, a sleek gray Siamese, leaped onto the table.

Roberto took out the library book, A History of Latinos in the United States.

Alice Thompson, the pitcher for the opposing team, took her place on the mound.

Directions   Identify the appositive phrase in each sentence. Write the phrase on the given line along with the word or words that it adds details or information about. The first sentence has been done for you.

1. The zoo is located in Green Park, a city preserve of about 100 acres.

   a city preserve of about 100 acres; Green Park

   _____

2. Carrie's mother drove us to the zoo in her car, a 2010 Honda Civic.

   a 2010 Honda Civic; car

   _____

3. The Monkey House, a huge building with 25 kinds of apes and monkeys,

   was our first stop.

   a huge building with 25 kinds of apes and monkeys;

   The Monkey House

4. Next we heard Professor Avery, an expert on birds of prey, give a lecture.

an expert on birds of prey; Professor Avery

5. We went to the snack bar and had some lunch, cheeseburgers, juice, and pieces of fruit, before we went to the petting zoo.

cheeseburgers, juice, and pieces of fruit; lunch

6. At the zoo we saw a llama, a four-footed animal that lives in South America.

a four-footed animal that lives in South America; llama

7. We also saw lions and other wild animals that live on the savannah, the vast grasslands in central Africa.

the vast grasslands in central Africa; savannah

8. I'm using the experience of our zoo visit for my next homework assignment, a four-page paper on a local landmark.

a four-page paper on a local landmark; next homework assignment

Next Step Write a paragraph about a local landmark—museum, sports arena, or other special place—in your town or city. Include am appositive phrase in each sentence. Identify the phrase and the word or words it gives information about to a partner.

Transitions

All writing should read smoothly and move clearly (logically) from one point to the next. Transitional or linking words like *also, finally,* and *later* and the repetition of key words or phrases can help make your writing smooth reading and clear. (See pages 572–573 in *Write Source* for a list of many different linking words.)

Directions — Many of the linking words have been taken out of the paragraph below. Read the paragraph and fill in each blank with a linking word or expression that helps the paragraph flow smoothly from one point to the next. Share your results.

1　　　When I was younger, I was always begging my parents to let

2　me cook. ___*Finally*___, my father said he'd teach me how to fry an egg.

3　___*First*___, we go out all the dishes, utensils, and food—frying pan,

4　pot holder, spatula, cup, plate, fork, eggs and margarine. ___*After*___

5　accidentally smashing one egg on the floor, I managed to crack an

6　egg into the cup. ___*Next*___, I heated margarine in the frying pan and

7　poured the egg into the pan. Flipping the egg over when it was done

8　on one side was hard. ___*Also*___, when it was time to lift the egg out of

9　the pan, I discovered how slippery fried eggs are. ___*After*___ a few tries,

10　I did manage to slide my over-easy egg onto the plate, but there was

11　nothing easy about it. ___*Finally*___, it was time to eat. *Even though* cooking

12　was more work than I had expected, that egg tasted great!

Next Step Write a paragraph telling how you made or put something together at school or home. Include transition words as you explain each step of the process. Share your paragraph by reading it aloud to a classmate.

Paragraph-to-Paragraph Coherence

Just like transitions within a paragraph, transition words and expressions link ideas between paragraphs and create paragraph-to-paragraph coherence. Transitions help form a logical chain from one idea to another in your writing, giving it focus and allowing your reader to follow your train of thought easily.

 Directions The transition words and phrases have been removed from the paragraphs below. Read the personal essay and fill in each blank with the best correct linking word or expression. The first one is done for you.

My friends and I have talked about getting a bike trail through our town for a long time. But we've never done anything about it. One day, our social studies teacher, Mr. Adams, told us we should take the matter before the Town Council and see if they would consider it. We had no idea how to go about this.

_____*However*_____, Mr. Adams said he'd be willing to help us. He explained that each monthly meeting of the Town Council begins with a public forum. Citizens can speak to the council about issues that concern them. He told us we should write down our ideas and shape them into short speeches we could deliver at the Town Council meeting.

_____*After*_____ our meeting with Mr. Adams, we went to work. Each of us wrote a short speech to bring to the public forum. Because we would only have a few minutes to talk, we kept our speeches brief and to the point. We cut out any unnecessary words and checked our work for spelling and grammar.

_____*Before*_____ going to the public forum, Mr. Adams suggested that we read our speeches to the class. We agreed to do so. It gave us confidence speaking before our fellow students and afterwards, our friends gave us constructive criticism on how we could improve both our writing and our delivery.

_____*As a result*_____, when we appeared at the public forum our speeches were highly effective. The council members listened attentively to every word. When we finished, they commended all of us for giving such a well-spoken presentation.

_____*Although*_____ the council members gave us no final answer on the question of a town bike trail, they took the idea seriously. They even formed a special committee to investigate the matter and asked two of us to serve on the committee.

_____*Finally*_____, after all this time, it looks like a bike trail through town is a definite possibility. And all because Mr. Adams urged us to speak out. We did and, to our surprise, it made a difference!

Sentence Fragments

A sentence is more than a random collection of words and phrases, just as an airplane is more than a pile of parts and pieces. (Neither will "fly" with parts missing.) A sentence must contain a subject and a predicate, which are arranged with other words to form a complete thought. A sentence that does not express a complete thought is called a **sentence fragment.** (See pages 503 and 504 in *Write Source* for more information about fragments.)

Examples

Sentence Fragment:
Are slender and furry.
(A subject is missing.)

Complete Sentence:
Otters **are slender and furry.**
(A subject has been added.)

Sentence Fragment:
The furry otter.
(A predicate is missing.)

Complete Sentence:
The furry otter is related to the weasel.
(A predicate has been added.)

Directions Identify the following groups of words with an "S" for each sentence or an "F" for each fragment. The first one has been done for you.

_F_ **1.** The otter's oily fur, which forms a waterproof coat.

_S_ **2.** River otters, once common in North America, are rarely seen.

_F_ **3.** Are afraid of humans.

_S_ **4.** Chattering noisily, they take turns sliding down snowy or muddy banks and belly flopping into the water.

_S_ **5.** Webbed toes and strong tails make otters excellent swimmers.

_F_ **6.** Paddling with their feet and using their strong tails to steer.

_F_ **7.** Prized for their rich fur like their relative the mink.

_S_ **8.** In the 1880s, otters were trapped heavily and began disappearing.

_F_ **9.** Are now a protected species with many programs to help them.

Comma Splices and Run-Ons 1

A **comma splice** occurs when you incorrectly connect two simple sentences with a comma instead of a period, semicolon, or connecting word.

A **run-on sentence** occurs when you incorrectly join two simple sentences without using any punctuation. (A period, a semicolon, or a comma and a coordinating conjunction are ways of correcting run-ons.) Both comma splices and run-on sentences can be avoided if you carefully review each of your sentences before sharing your writing with your readers. (For more information, see page 506 in *Write Source*.)

Example

Comma Splice:
Bamboo is a giant form of grass, its shoots are a tasty vegetable.

Run-On:
Bamboo is a giant form of grass its shoots are a tasty vegetable.

Corrected Sentences:
Bamboo is a giant form of grass. Its shoots are a tasty vegetable. (or)
Bamboo is a giant form of grass, and its shoots are a tasty vegetable.

 Directions Place a "CS" in front of each comma splice, an "RO" in front of each run-on sentence, and a "C" in front of each correct sentence. Correct each faulty sentence. The first sentence has been done for you.

(Answers may vary.)

CS 1. Bamboo is definitely one of the most interesting plants,ₐ *and* it is
    valued for its beauty and usefulness.

C 2. Bamboo may be one of the world's most useful plants.

RO 3. Bamboo grows in huge groves. it serves as a natural buffer
    against floods and erosion.

C 4. In addition, bamboo enriches the soil.

RO   **5.** People have found bamboo indispensable they use it for buildings, for musical instruments, and for furniture.

CS   **6.** Bamboo is also an important food source, its crisp texture makes it a favorite ingredient in Asian cooking.

C   **7.** Bamboo is interesting not only to ordinary people, but it is also interesting to scientists.

RO   **8.** This plant is a member of the grass family, it grows naturally on every continent except Europe and Antarctica.

C   **9.** About a thousand different species of bamboo exist, differing widely in color, shape, and size.

CS   **10.** Bamboo varies greatly in size, some varieties grow to the height of field grass while others reach heights of more than 100 feet.

C   **11.** All bamboo plants have stalks known as *culms*.

CS   **12.** The culm is usually round, hollow, and jointed, it makes the plant unusually strong.

RO   **13.** One of the most interesting features of bamboo is its growth speed, nothing grows as tall and as rapidly as bamboo.

C   **14.** In Japan, a common type of bamboo is known to have grown three feet in 24 hours.

RO   **15.** At this rate, the stalk's growth would likely be visible an observer, however, would have to be extremely patient.

Next Step Sometimes it's easier to catch sentence errors in someone else's writing than in your own. (You are, in a sense, too close to your own work.) Exchange a piece of writing in progress with a classmate and check each other's work for comma splices and run-on sentences.

Comma Splices and Run-Ons 2

Combining several related thoughts into the same sentence can be a good thing. You just need to avoid two pitfalls: **run-on sentences** and **comma splices.** Enthusiastic or fast writers often make these errors in their early drafts, but careful editing can correct these problems. Experiment with different punctuation—periods, semicolons—and different connecting, words —*and, but, nor, or, yet, for*—to get the effect you want. (See page 506 in *Write Source* for more information.)

Examples

Incorrect:
He swung at the ball, he missed it.

Correct:
He swung at the ball; he missed it.
He swung at the ball, but he missed it.
He swung at the ball. He missed it.

 Directions In the groups of words below, place a "CS" before each comma splice and an "RO" before each run-on sentence. Then correct each error. If a sentence is correct, place a "C" before the sentence. The first one has been done for you. *(Answers may vary.)*

___CS___ **1.** Some people are afraid of spiders, other people think they are a sign of good luck.

___RO___ **2.** Most spiders are strange-looking creatures, *but* most aren't harmful to people.

___RO___ **3.** Spiders are often used in monster films, these spiders are huge.

___CS___ **4.** Spiders have eight eyes, they have eight legs, too.

___RO___ **5.** Spiders have fangs. most have poisonous fangs to paralyze their prey.

_C_ **6.** Not every spider spins webs, but each one has spinnerets, which allows it to spin fine silk threads.

_RO_ **7.** Silk is used by different types of spiders for different things it can be used for webs and for wrapping victims.

_C_ **8.** Baby spiders of some species (called "parachuters") spin long thin threads and are carried away by the wind, scattering over a wide area.

_RO_ **9.** The trap-door spider actually makes a hinged door it digs a hole in the ground and closes the door over the hole.

_C_ **10.** The California trap-door spider is so strong that it can resist a force 38 times its weight.

_CS_ **11.** Black widow spiders can actually be deadly their bites can cause illness and sometimes even death to humans.

_CS_ **12.** The most venomous spider is the Brazilian huntsman it often hides in people's shoes.

_RO_ **13.** The largest spider ever found had a leg span of 11 inches the smallest spider was the size of a period on this page.

_C_ **14.** Why do some spiders buzz and others purr?

Next Step How do you feel about spiders? Write a paragraph describing your personal feelings about spiders. Use your own paper.

Sentence Problems Review 1

Good sentences are essential to good writing. In order to write good sentences, you need to avoid some basic sentence errors. Three of the more common sentence errors are **run-on sentences, comma splices,** and **sentence fragments.** (See *Write Source* pages 503–504 and 506 to review these errors, or look back to specific exercises you have already completed on each type of error.)

> **Directions**
>
> Place an "RO" in front of each run-on sentence that follows. Place a "CS" in front of each comma splice and an "F" before each sentence fragment. Then fix each error. The first one has been done for you.
>
> *(Answers may vary.)*

RO   **1.** Last night, Sam and I biked to the arena to see Garbage in concert ; it was a very interesting ride.

F   **2.** Our route through downtown traffic was congested .

CS   **3.** Biking soon became tricky ; the roads were jammed with traffic heading for the concert.

F   **4.** Impatient drivers were blowing their car horns.

CS   **5.** Sam was really nervous about all the traffic ; he wasn't used to bumper-to-bumper cars.

F   **6.** The traffic was More like New York City than Madison, Wisconsin.

CS   **7.** We were riding in the bike lane. Cars kept edging over toward us.

RO   **8.** We finally made it to the arena. Sam confessed he had been worried we wouldn't make it.

F   **9.** We were Sitting so far back that the musicians looked like ants.

RO   **10.** The sound was great, though. We probably heard better than the people in the front row.

Sentence Problems Review 2

Directions Put an "RO" in front of any run-on sentences that follow, a "CS" in front of any comma splices, and an "F" in front of any fragments. Then fix each error. (Refer to pages 503–504 and 506 in *Write Source* for explanations and examples.) *(Answers may vary.)*

__CS__ 1. My dad is a long-time member of our town's volunteer fire
department, he also belongs to our local rescue squad. (or) .H
6 /;

__F__ 2. He is ∧Always getting called to a fire or an accident right in the
middle of supper or when his favorite football team is playing
on television.

__RO__ 3. One night he rescued two kittens from a burning barn and
brought them home. we named the kittens Sparky and Soot. W

__F__ 4. We ∧Still have both kittens 10 years later.

__CS__ 5. The kittens are all grown up now, they have become regular T
members of our family. 6

__RO__ 6. I'll never forget the night we got Sparky and Soot they were (or) .T
cold and smelled like smoke. ∧;

__F__ 7. Tiny heads were ∧poking out of the pockets of my dad's big rubber
coat.

__CS__ 8. I thought they were toys, I heard them meow. then
6 /;

__F__ 9. For a child, are ∧there many things cuter than baby kittens?

__RO__ 10. My sister and I loved the kittens we took them up in our tree (or) .W
house and everywhere we went. ∧;

Rambling Sentences

Just as you should correct any fragments, run-ons, or comma splices in your writing, you should also be careful not to use too many *and*'s or *but*'s. The result could be a series of rambling sentences. (See page 507 in *Write Source* for more information.)

Directions   In the following passage (a rewritten scene from *The Adventures of Tom Sawyer* by Mark Twain), look for sentences that ramble on and on. Fix them by taking out some (but not all) of the *and*'s, *but*'s, or *so*'s. Also, add punctuation and capitalization as needed.

(Answers may vary.)

1   Tom typically carried treasures in his pocket, but this particular

2   Sunday, the "pinch bug" (a large black beetle with formidable jaws) was

3   taken out. and the beetle helped himself to Tom's finger and was thereby

4   flicked into the church aisle. but a poodle, in church with his master,

5   saw the bug, came up to it, and started to play with it. and the poodle's

6   chin got too close. and the chin was seized, there was a yelp, and the

7   pinch bug went flying farther down the aisle. so the poodle moved

8   toward the beetle, became distracted by a fly, forgot about the beetle

9   entirely and sat down on it. and with a wild yelp, the dog went

10   streaking up the aisle like a woolly comet. In desperation, the dog

11   jumped on his master's lap and was flung out of a nearby window. and

12   people snickered, the sermon ended, and Tom went home quite satisfied

13   except for one thing. he didn't mind that the dog had played with his

14   pinch bug, but he did not think it right of the dog to carry it off.

Next Step Write a paragraph about a memorable animal experience. Exchange first drafts with a classmate. Check each other's writing for any rambling sentences and checkmark those sentences that need to be rewritten. Return the papers and make corrections as necessary.

Wordiness

In a popular book about writing entitled *Elements of Style*, the authors stress the importance of clear writing. They explain that you write clearly by removing unnecessary words or phrases.

Example

Wordy Sentence:
I kept thinking about all the things I needed to remember to take along for tomorrow's fishing trip—my lures, the rods, the bait.

Clearer Sentence:
I kept thinking about everything I needed for tomorrow's trip—my lures, rods, bait.

Directions   Read the model paragraph and cross out any words that you think are unnecessary. (Some sentences can be corrected in more than one way.)
(Answers may vary.)

   (1) It was late—time to go to sleep if we wanted to get up ~~early~~ at 4:00 a.m. ~~in the morning~~ for some good fishing. (2) But we needed worms and were too excited to sleep ~~which goes without saying~~. (3) We carefully slid the patio door open ~~with great care~~, trying hard to keep quiet ~~and not make any noise either~~. (4) There was a light fog that seemed to cling to everything ~~it touched~~. (5) Closing the door slowly, we stepped softly onto the patio. (6) My friend, ~~he~~ turned on his flashlight ~~so we could see better in the haze~~. (7) We found the worm box on the garage shelf and headed for the flower garden, ~~walking toward it from the garage~~. (8) I flashed my flashlight at the moist ground and spotted a couple of fat night crawlers slipping back into their holes ~~and sliding under the ground to escape~~. (9) My friend grabbed them just in time and dropped them into the box. (10) On we went, shining our lights and grabbing worms until we had plenty of bait ~~that would be enough~~ for a morning of fishing. (11) ~~My friend and I,~~ W we were tired as we put everything away and sneaked back to our room, finally ready to get some rest before our fishing trip.

Next Step Check at least one of your most recent writings and eliminate any unnecessary words you may have included.

Double Negatives and Incorrect Usage

As you talk with your friends, you'll probably hear a lot of *nonstandard language.* What is natural in spoken language can be confusing in written communication.

Though double negatives are common in song lyrics and casual speech, you should avoid them when writing, unless you are quoting someone or creating an informal sentence. (See page 510 in *Write Source* for more information.)

This is a test. This is o

Examples

Incorrect:

We don't need no money.
(Does this mean "We don't need money" or "We need money"?)

Correct:

We don't need any money.
(The meaning—"We don't need money"—is clear.)

Incorrect:

I didn't barely pass the test.
(Does this sentence mean "I did pass"? Or does it mean "I didn't pass"?)

Correct:

I barely passed the test.
(The meaning—"I passed the test"—is clear.)

Note: Do not use *hardly, barely,* or *scarcely* with a negative word; the result is a double negative.

> **Directions** — Write the correct negative for each sentence below. The first one has been done for you.

1. There _____*is hardly any*_____ time to practice before the soccer game.
   (isn't hardly no, is hardly any)

2. Chocolate can poison canines, so never to give _____*any*_____ to your dog.
   (any, none)

3. We don't need _____*any*_____ heroes—just a few true friends.
   (no, any)

4. Antarctica doesn't have _____*any*_____ of the food plants of other climates.
(none, any)

5. Antarctica's ice contains algae that _____*are no*_____ bigger than a single cell.
(aren't no, are no)

6. Shrimplike krill, _____*scarcely bigger*_____ than the single-celled
(scarcely no bigger, scarcely bigger)

plants, eat the algae and become part of the food chain that supports

whales, penguins, and seals.

7. I can't think of _____*anything*_____ better than living on a houseboat.
(nothing, anything)

8. Our parrot doesn't say _____*any*_____ words, but he mimics the sounds of
(no, any)

our dishwasher, our telephone, and the family cat!

9. Aaron didn't have _____*any*_____ money for a boat, so he made a raft.
(no, any)

10. Scarcely _____*anybody*_____ showed up to audition for the school play.
(nobody, anybody)

11. Later that year, so many people tried out for *West Side Story* that we

_____*could hardly*_____ all cram into the practice gym.
(couldn't hardly, could hardly)

12. Ann didn't want _____*any*_____ part of Jake's plan to put sea monkeys in
(no, any)

Miss Han's classroom aquarium.

Next Step Collect several examples of standard and nonstandard language from magazines, TV, and the radio. Jot them down on a sheet of paper. Explain why each example is an appropriate (or inappropriate) piece for its intended audience and purpose.

Misplaced Modifiers

Modifiers are words, phrases, and clauses that describe the simple subject or simple predicate of the sentence. The key to using modifiers effectively is to make sure that you place them as close as possible to the words they modify. Misplacing the modifier makes a sentence confusing and sometimes silly. (See page 505 in *Write Source* to examine misplaced modifiers in more detail.)

Example

Confusing Sentence:
John Glenn returned to space shortly after turning 77 **on October 29, 1998.**
(It sounds as if John Glenn turned 77 on October 29, 1998.)

Clear Sentence:
Shortly after turning 77, **John Glenn returned to space on October 29, 1998.**

 Directions Rewrite the following sentences to correct the misplaced modifiers. The first one has been done for you.

1. John Glenn relaxed on the day before the flight with his family.

   On the day before the flight, John Glenn relaxed with his family.

2. He was eager to begin his second flight into space with all the media in attendance.

   With all the media in attendance, he was eager to begin his second

   flight into space.

3. After being away from flight for many years, the new space program was an opportunity that Glenn couldn't resist.

   After being away from flight for many years, Glenn couldn't resist an

   opportunity like the new space program.

4. The space crew spent the morning adjusting their bulky space suits along with John Glenn.

The space crew, along with John Glenn, spent the morning adjusting

their bulky space suits.

5. Because he's the oldest American astronaut to fly in space, one reporter decided to publish a book about John Glenn and his flight.

Because John Glenn is the oldest American astronaut to fly in space,

one reporter decided to publish a book about him and his flight.

6. Many local residents were able to watch the launch of the space shuttle from their own backyards.

From their own backyards, many local residents were able to watch

the launch of the space shuttle.

7. Wearing bulky space suits, the ground crew helped the astronauts board the shuttle.

Wearing bulky space suits, the astronauts boarded the shuttle with

the help of the ground crew.

8. The president of the United States came to watch the space shuttle lift off with a congressional delegation.

The president of the United States, with a congressional delegation,

came to watch the space shuttle lift off.

Next Step John Glenn was the first U.S. astronaut to orbit the earth. Using the Internet or other research tools, find out more about him and his career. Then write a paragraph about your findings. Read your paragraph aloud to a classmate and ask him or her to check your writing for misplaced modifiers.

Subject-Verb Agreement 1

The subject and the verb of a sentence must agree in number. In other words, if the subject is singular, the verb must be singular, too. If the subject is plural, then the verb must be plural. (See pages 508 and 509 in *Write Source* for more information and examples.)

Examples

Compound Subjects:

Annie and her roommate are riding to the concert in our van.

(Compound subjects connected by "and" need a plural verb.)

Neither Annie nor her friends are riding home with us.

(With compound subjects connected by "or" or "nor," the verb must agree with the subject nearest to the verb.)

Collective Noun Subjects:

Camp staff report for duty a week before camp begins.

("Staff" is plural because each member will be coming from a different place.)

This staff is the best group of counselors in Camp Gichagoomie's history.

(The members of the staff are referred to as one group, so the verb is singular.)

 Directions Write the correct form of the verb in the sentences below. The first sentence has been done for you.

1. A skunk and its enemy _____*are*_____ soon parted.
   _____(is, are)_____

2. The crew _____*eat*_____ in groups of four between 11:30 a.m. and 1:30 p.m.
   _____(eats, eat)_____

3. Beans and Barley Restaurant _____*serves*_____ great veggie burgers.
   _____(serve, serves)_____

4. Neither the weather nor the traffic _____*was*_____ to blame for the accident.
   _____(was, were)_____

5. Either math or pre-algebra _____*is*_____ a requirement for eighth graders.
(is, are)

6. Congress rarely _____*completes*_____ its agenda before it adjourns.
(complete, completes)

7. Cotton candy, carnival rides, and fireworks _____*make*_____ state fairs fun.
(makes, make)

8. The Cornhuskers and the Jayhawks _____*are*_____ bound to meet in the Big
(is, are)

Eight conference play-offs this year.

9. Your mother, father, or legal guardian _____*is*_____ required to sign your
(is, are)

permission slip.

10. The Summerfest crowd _____*was*_____ disbanding when the rain started.
(was, were)

11. Each twin _____*faces*_____ challenges as one or the other makes new friends.
(faces, face)

12. Neither the faculty nor the students _____*were*_____ happy with the old gym.
(was, were)

13. The committee _____*has*_____ recommended improvements for school lunches.
(has, have)

14. Buses and bicycles _____*share*_____ the credit for reducing air pollution.
(shares, share)

15. The little pig who built his house of bricks claimed that work and play

_____*don't*_____ mix!
(doesn't, don't)

Next Step As a class, talk about examples of subject-verb agreement that seem tricky or confusing. Then write a tricky sentence—possibly similar to one you've discussed. Next write a rule that will help you remember how to figure out whether the verb should be singular or plural in sentences like the one you've composed.

Subject-Verb Agreement 2

Figuring out whether a verb should be singular (to agree with a singular subject) or plural (to agree with a plural subject) can be tricky! Check out the examples and rules on pages 475, 508, and 509 in *Write Source* before completing the exercise below.

Examples

Subject Separated from the Verb:

I myself, not my friends, am responsible for the decisions I make.

(Make sure the subject and verb are in agreement.)

Subject Follows the Verb:

Piled on the table was a week's harvest of beans from Grandma's garden.

(Make sure the "true" subject and the verb agree.)

Indefinite Pronouns:

Everyone needs someone to talk to.

(The following indefinite pronouns require a singular verb: *each, either, neither, one, everyone, anyone, everybody, everything, someone, somebody, anybody, anything, nobody,* and *another.*)

Most of the ghost stories were scary, but none were truly frightening.

(The following indefinite pronouns can be either singular or plural: *all, any, most, none, some.* Check the noun the pronoun stands for to decide whether you need a singular or a plural verb.)

 Directions Write the correct form of the verb in each sentence below. The first sentence has been done for you.

1. Everyone in a traditional Chinese family _____*has*_____ three names, and
    (has, have)

    each of those names is written using one character.

2. Each of the characters, which look like pictures, _____*stands*_____ for a
    (stands, stand)

    particular part of the person's name.

3. The family name, followed by the person's given name, ___**is**___ written

   (is, are)

   first.

4. Some names ___**have**___ a couple brush strokes, while others have many.

   (has, have)

5. A Chinese phone book, quite different from English, Spanish, or German

   directories, ___**lists**___ names according to the number of brush strokes in

   (lists, list)

   the character representing the family name.

6. The names represented by the simplest characters with only a few brush

   strokes ___**are**___ listed near the beginning of the directory.

   (is, are)

7. Anyone with a name requiring many brush strokes ___**has**___ to look for

   (has, have)

   his or her listing near the end of the directory.

8. Everybody who wants to look up friends in the phone book ___**has**___ to

   (has, have)

   remember more than 3,000 individual characters!

9. Perhaps anyone who grows up learning each word with a picture ___**finds**___

   (finds, find)

   remembering Chinese characters as easy as remembering how a word sounds.

10. There ___**are**___ a number of other languages that use characters instead

    (is, are)

    of letters, but Chinese is the most complex.

Next Step If you have problems remembering which indefinite pronouns are singular and which are plural, create a list for each type. Then use the first letters of the pronouns in each list to create an acronym to help you remember them as either singular or plural.

Subject-Verb Agreement 3

Subjects and verbs must agree in number in your sentences. A singular subject needs a singular verb. (The *book is* hidden.) Plural subjects require plural verbs. (The *books are* hidden.) It's also important to know which indefinite pronouns need a singular verb. Pronouns like *each, one,* and *everyone* require singular verbs. (See pages 475, 508, and 509 in *Write Source* for more information.)

Examples

Each of the boys hopes to find a fossil.

Either is capable of finding bones just like paleontologist Othniel Marsh.

Neither Jon nor Sherman expects to find a Brontosaurus bone.

 Directions In the following short paragraph, underline the subjects with a single line and their verbs with two lines. The first sentence has been done for you.

1   For a long time, no one realized that the Apatosaurus and the

2   Brontosaurus were the same dinosaur. Different sets of dinosaur bones

3   were found in different places in Wyoming and were thought to be from

4   different dinosaurs. The first skeleton discovered had no skull. The

5   American scientist Othniel Marsh named it Apatosaurus. Two years later,

6   scientists found a more complete skeleton. Marsh named it Brontosaurus.

7   Eventually, everyone realized that these two dinosaurs were the same. One

8   of the names—Apatosaurus—has become formally accepted and is used by

9   paleontologists. One of the names—Brontosaurus, the thunder lizard—

10   seems to be more popular with the general public.

Subject-Verb Agreement 4

If the subject of a sentence is separated from its verb by other words or phrases, you may be tempted to make the verb agree with the closest noun—which is not necessarily the subject. One way to avoid this problem is to say the sentence aloud without the words that come between the subject and the verb. Try this technique on the examples below. (Also, see pages 508–509 and 728.1 in *Write Source* for more information.)

Examples

The <u>raptors</u> in the time of dinosaurs <u>were</u> fast and able hunters.

Fossil <u>eggs</u> found in the desert <u>prove</u> dinosaur mothers put their eggs in nests.

 Directions Read the sentences below. Then rewrite the sentences, separating the subject and the verb with a phrase. The first one has been done for you.

(Answers will vary.)

1. <u>Raptors</u> <u>were</u> hungry all the time.

   Raptors feeding on small animals were hungry all the time.

2. <u>Dinosaurs</u> <u>lived</u> millions of years ago.

   _____

   _____

3. <u>Fossils</u> <u>tell</u> us about dinosaurs.

   _____

4. Some <u>dinosaurs</u> <u>were</u> bigger than houses.

   _____

   _____

5. <u>Tyrannosaurus Rex</u> <u>was</u> the biggest meat eater.

   _____

   _____

Subject-Verb Agreement Review

> **Directions** In the following sentences, write the correct verb form in the blank and draw an arrow from the verb to its subject.

1. The first people to use concrete for most of their public buildings ___were___
   (was, were)

   the Romans.

2. Today, contractors ___use___ concrete for many purposes.
   (uses, use)

3. Sidewalks and streets in many cities ___are___ concrete.
   (is, are)

4. Most homeowners ___prefer___ durable concrete driveways.
   (prefers, prefer)

5. A house builder using proper equipment ___casts___ concrete to look like brick.
   (casts, cast)

6. Sometimes a contractor or a homeowner ___adds___ color to the concrete.
   (adds, add)

7. With steel reinforcing rods, concrete buildings ___withstand___ the
   (withstands, withstand)

   shock from an earthquake.

8. Under most houses with a basement ___is___ a concrete floor.
   (is, are)

9. Brick or wood, alternatives to concrete, ___is___ usually more expensive.
   (is, are)

10. Most of the airport runways in this country ___are___ concrete.
    (is, are)

11. In many towns in tornado alley, there ___are___ concrete storm shelters.
    (is, are)

12. The staff of the high school ___patrols___ five concrete playgrounds.
    (patrols, patrol)

Sentence Problems Review 3

Directions Read the paragraph below. It contains a number of words, phrases, and sentences that are unclear and could easily mislead the reader. Find one example of each type of error listed beneath the paragraph; write the number of the sentence in which you found each error on the blank provided. (See pages 503–510 in *Write Source* for help.) Then correct each error in the paragraph itself. (Rewrite the one sentence that needs major revising on the lines provided.)

(1) Learning to pilot a Superflooz VII Intergalactic Spacezipper at warp speed is really much easier than it sounds. (2) First, the pilot must strap into the control seat so he or she ~~can't~~ *can* hardly move. (3) Then he *or she* must switch on the viewing screen. (4) This special screen ~~nearly~~ allows the pilot to see for *nearly* 500 miles. (5) At this point, the pilot must switch on the Magno-Zip Atombooster. (6) This switch is located just above the pilot's head and looks sort of like a radish. (7) One of the switches ~~are~~ *is* green and should not be touched at all, for it will activate the ship's destruct mechanism. (8) ~~After warming up for three minutes, the pilot can throw the switch for the Magno-Zip Atombooster to the no-return position.~~ (9) The pilot must remember not to overload ~~their~~ *his or her* Magno-Zip Atombooster. (10) If the pilot follows ~~one~~ *all* of these directions carefully, the trip should be a smooth one.

_____2_____ Double negative   _3, 9, 10_ Pronoun problem (agreement)

_____4_____ Misplaced modifier (one word)   ___8___ Misplaced modifier (phrase)

_____7_____ Agreement of subject and verb

Revised Sentence: *(8) After warming up the Magno-Zip Atombooster for three minutes, the pilot can throw the switch to the no-return position.*

Combining Sentences Using Key Words

Sometimes a single word can make a world of difference in a sentence. One added key word can provide just the extra touch needed to add impact to your sentence. If you have used two sentences to explain something, it's always a good idea to see if you can combine the two sentences by "borrowing" a key word from one and adding it to the other. Combining sentences by using key words can help you create more concise, mature sentences.

Examples

Combining with an Adjective:
John's brother nibbles "munchies" between meals. He is <u>younger</u> than John.
John's younger brother nibbles "munchies" between meals.

Combining with a Participle:
Ji's dog scares people. Ji's dog <u>snarls</u>.
Ji's snarling dog scares people.
(*Snarls* has been changed to its participle form.)

Combining with an Adverb:
I passed my English test. I passed it <u>yesterday</u>.
Yesterday, I passed my English test.

 Directions In each pair of sentences, underline the key word(s) in the second sentence and then move the form of that word (indicated in parentheses) to the first sentence.

1. Eligia did the exercises with ease. The exercises were <u>difficult</u>. *(adjective)*

   Eligia did the difficult exercises with ease.

2. I have to mow my overgrown lawn. I will mow the lawn <u>later</u>. *(adverb)*

   I have to mow my overgrown lawn later.

3. The fans stormed onto the field. The fans <u>screamed</u>. *(participle)*

   The screaming fans stormed onto the field.

4. Juan wrote an essay on endangered species. It <u>amazed</u> everyone. *(participle)*

Juan wrote an amazing essay on endangered species.

5. Jeison loves salsa. He loves it <u>hot</u> and <u>spicy</u>. *(adjective)*

Jeison loves hot and spicy salsa.

6. The crowd loved the play. The crowd <u>cheered</u>. *(participle)*

The cheering crowd loved the play.

7. I lost my wallet at the movies. I lost it <u>last week</u>. *(adverb)*

I lost my wallet at the movies last week.

8. The sun made me squint. The sun was <u>setting</u>. *(participle)*

The setting sun made me squint.

9. I changed the flat tire on the side of the road. I changed it <u>quickly</u>. *(adverb)*

I quickly changed the flat tire on the side of the road.

10. Bill's basket saved the game for us. He made it at the <u>last minute</u>. *(compound adjective)*

Bill's last-minute basket saved the game for us.

Next Step Write five pairs of sentences suitable for key word combining. Exchange your sentences with a classmate. Each of you should combine the sentences you received.

Combining Sentences with a Series of Words or Phrases

Being able to combine shorter sentences into longer sentences is a very valuable writing skill to learn. Longer sentences can help you show relationships that are hard to express in shorter sentences. To effectively combine short sentences, you need to recognize what the shorter sentences have in common—what series of words, phrases, or ideas can be pulled together into one longer sentence. Study the examples below. (Also turn to pages 512 and 513 in *Write Source* for more examples.)

Examples

Shorter Sentences:
Aaron skies on snow.
He skies on water.
He skies on ice.

Combined Sentence Using a Series of Words:
Aaron skies on snow, water, and ice.

Shorter Sentences:
Aaron sprained his ankle.
He bruised his hip.
He wrenched his back.

Combined Sentence Using a Series of Phrases:
Aaron sprained his ankle, bruised his hip, and wrenched his back.

 Directions | Combine the following sets of short sentences into longer ones using the method asked for in parentheses. The first one has been done for you.

1. John tore down the hill. He cut in front of Aaron. He caused him to fall. *(Use a series of phrases.)*

   John tore down the hill, cut in front of Aaron, and caused him to fall.

2. As Aaron tried to get out of John's way, he tumbled. Then he slid and spun. *(Use a series of words.)*

As Aaron tried to get out of John's way, he tumbled, slid, and spun.

3. John was skiing too fast. He was moving carelessly from side to side. He was taking unnecessary chances. *(Use a series of phrases.)*

John was skiing too fast, moving carelessly from side to side, and

taking unnecessary chances.

4. As John skied past Aaron, he whistled. He shouted and laughed. *(Use a series of words.)*

John whistled, shouted, and laughed as he skied past Aaron.

5. The ski patrol headed up the hill with their toboggan. They brought a back brace. They also brought an inflatable leg cast. *(Use a series of phrases.)*

The ski patrol headed up the hill with their toboggan, a back brace,

and an inflatable leg cast.

6. Aaron now sits by himself. He watches hockey on television and dreams of getting back on the slopes. *(Use a series of phrases.)*

Aaron now sits by himself, watches hockey on television, and dreams

of getting back on the slopes.

Next Step Write a paragraph describing an accident (or near accident) you have had. Then rewrite the paragraph to see how many sentences you can combine using a series of words or phrases as you did above. Compare your two paragraphs. Which one reads better?

Combining Sentences with Compound Subjects and Predicates

Sentences are not limited to having a single subject and predicate (or verb). A sentence can have two or more subjects called a **compound subject.** A sentence can also have a **compound predicate.** Some sentences may have both a compound subject and a compound predicate. Sometimes, instead of writing two short sentences, you may want to combine the subjects or predicates (or both) into a single sentence providing the same information. (See page 515 in *Write Source*.)

Note: Notice how using a compound predicate to combine the two sentences below eliminates repetition and lets you use one sentence instead of two.

Example

Shorter Sentences:
I got up at 6:00 in the morning.
I got dressed in my warmest clothes.

Combined Sentence Using a Compound Predicate:
I got up at 6:00 in the morning and dressed in my warmest clothes.

 Directions Combine each of the following pairs of sentences into a single sentence that uses compound subjects or predicates. See page 515 in *Write Source* for more information and additional examples. Some sentences may require both a compound subject and compound predicate. The first sentence has been done for you.

1. My dad was taking me ice fishing. My uncle was coming, too.

   My dad and my uncle were taking me ice fishing.

2. My dad made me a huge pancake-and-sausage breakfast. He asked if I was full.

   My dad made me a huge pancake-and-sausage breakfast and asked

   if I was full.

3. On the way to the lake, the two men told funny fishing stories. They poked fun at each other's fish tales.

On the way to the lake, the two men told funny fishing stories and

poked fun at each other's fish tales.

4. I believed only about half the stories. I laughed at all of them anyway.

I believed only about half the stories but laughed at all of them

anyway.

5. The heat in the car made me drowsy. The car's heat finally put me to sleep.

The heat in the car made me drowsy and finally put me to sleep.

6. At the lake, the cold wind cut right through my warm clothes. It caused my teeth to start chattering.

At the lake, the cold wind cut right through my warm clothes

and caused my teeth to start chattering.

7. My dad gathered kindling. My uncle helped and soon started a hot blazing fire.

My dad and uncle gathered kindling and soon started a hot blazing

fire.

8. I liked fishing that day. I enjoyed the warm fire even more.

I liked fishing that day but enjoyed the warm fire even more.

Next Step Write a paragraph describing an experience you have had in nature. Then rewrite the paragraph, combining sentences using compound subjects and predicates. Compare your two paragraphs and discuss the results with a classmate. Do each of you see an improvement in your rewritten versions?

Kinds of Sentences

Sentences can be distinguished by their purpose. Some sentences ask questions (**interrogative**), some are statements (**declarative**), some give commands (**imperative**), and some are exclamations (**exclamatory**). As a writer, you choose the kind of sentence you want based on the message you want to give to the reader. (See page 518 in *Write Source* to examine the four kinds of sentences in more detail.)

Examples

Declarative Sentence:
Tornadoes are among the most destructive natural disasters.

Imperative Sentence:
Head for shelter immediately when a tornado warning is issued.

Interrogative Sentence:
Do you know where the safest place in your home is during a tornado?

Exclamatory Sentence:
The tornado caused millions of dollars of damage in just three minutes!

 Directions Label each of the following sentences as "declarative," "imperative," "interrogative," or "exclamatory." Then add the correct end punctuation. The first one has been done for you.

declarative **1.** Tornadoes occur most often in the Plains States during the spring and summer.

exclamatory **2.** Tornado wind speeds can reach over 300 miles per hour!

imperative **3.** To protect yourself, learn all you can about tornadoes.

declarative **4.** The most violent tornadoes have more than one vortex or rotating center.

interrogative **5.** Did you know that in Mississippi three 40-passenger buses were tossed over an eight-foot embankment during a tornado?

interrogative	**6.**	Was anyone injured in the accident?
exclamatory	**7.**	No, incredibly, no one was injured!
imperative	**8.**	Stay away from windows and open spaces during a tornado.
interrogative	**9.**	Have you heard of "Tornado Alley"?
declarative	**10.**	This is an area between Nebraska and central Texas where tornadoes are most likely to occur.
declarative	**11.**	Most tornadoes happen during the month of May, but the most deadly ones occur in April.
imperative	**12.**	If you find yourself in an open field during a tornado, find a low spot immediately.
exclamatory	**13.**	A tornado can drive a piece of straw through a wooden post!
declarative	**14.**	Tornadoes are most common in the United States, the former Soviet Union, and Australia.
interrogative	**15.**	If you are driving your car and the radio warns of a tornado in the area, what should you do?
exclamatory	**16.**	Auntie Em, Auntie Em, it's a twister!

Next Step Tornadoes, hurricanes, and earthquakes are frightening natural disasters. With a classmate, devise a safety plan for your home to deal with the natural disaster most likely to occur in your area of the country. Share that plan with your family. Be sure to check your writing for complete sentences.

Types of Sentences

Skilled writers vary the lengths of their sentences. Using too many short sentences makes writing choppy; however, using too many long sentences can make writing confusing. When you write, try to mix **simple, compound, complex,** and **compound-complex** sentences to achieve variety and clarity. (See pages 515–517 in *Write Source* for more on types of sentences.)

Examples

Simple Sentence:
Jack and Maria love in-line skating.

Compound Sentence:
They play on a roller-hockey team, and **they enjoy the competition**.

Complex Sentence:
Although they are amateurs now, Jack and Maria dream of being professional skaters someday.

Compound-Complex Sentence:
Because they are determined to fulfill their dream, Jack and Maria practice daily, and **they read everything that they can find about skating**.

Note: A compound-complex sentence contains two or more independent clauses and one or more dependent clauses.

 Directions Label the following sentences with "S" for simple, "C" for compound, "CX" for complex, and "CC" for compound-complex. The first sentence has been done for you.

_____S_____ **1.** Joseph Merlin, a Dutchman, invented roller skates in the eighteenth century.

_____CX_____ **2.** After he studied the design of ice skates, Joseph fastened wooden spools in the place of the ice-skate blades.

_CC_ **3.** In 1763, metal wheels replaced the wooden spools, and in 1863, American inventor James Leonard Plimpton created rocking skates that allowed the skater to maneuver more easily.

_C_ **4.** Ball-bearing wheels were introduced late in the nineteenth century, and, as a result, roller-skating became even more popular.

_S_ **5.** Skateboards and in-line skates are modifications of roller skates.

_S_ **6.** Skateboards are short, wide boards made of wood, plastic, or fiberglass.

_C_ **7.** In-line skates were first manufactured in the 1980s, and they have become very popular with people of all ages.

_CX_ **8.** Although roller-skating has not been accepted as an Olympic sport, athletes can compete in events like short-track speed skating with other roller skaters.

_CC_ **9.** Because Roller Derby was so popular in the 1950s, fans flocked to indoor rinks to watch, or they stayed home and watched on their televisions.

Next Step Find out more about Roller Derby, speed skating, or roller hockey by using the Internet or other sources. Write a paragraph about your findings and share your writing with a classmate. Ask your classmate to label the types of sentences you used in your paragraph.

Writing Complex Sentences 1

Sentence combining is one of the most valuable skills you can develop as a writer. With practice, you can combine short, choppy sentences into longer, smoother-reading sentences. One of the most efficient kinds of sentences to form when combining is the **complex sentence.** Complex sentences contain one independent clause and one or more dependent clauses. (See page 517 and 746.1 in *Write Source* for more information.)

Directions Combine the following short sentences by adding the subordinating conjunction indicated in the parentheses. The first one has been done for you.

1. Visitors have been coming to Vancouver Island for years. Few know about the excellent surfing locations. *(although)*

   Although visitors have been coming to Vancouver Island for years, few know

   about the excellent surfing locations.

2. The sun rose. Frank began to hike the trails. *(as soon as)*

   As soon as the sun rose, Frank began to hike the trails.

3. He planned to go hunting. He changed his plans so he could take his daughter skiing. *(although)*

   Although he planned to go hunting, he changed his plans so he could

   take his daughter skiing.

4. People keep very busy and very fit on Vancouver Island. There are many outdoor activities. *(because)*

   People keep very busy and very fit on Vancouver Island because there

   are many outdoor activities.

5. The hillsides are always green. It rains a lot on the coast. *(because)*

   The hillsides are always green because it rains a lot on the coast.

6. Residents of Vancouver Island are always prepared for rain or sunshine. The weather is unpredictable. *(because)*

   Because the weather is unpredictable, residents of Vancouver Island

   are always prepared for rain or sunshine.

7. Kayakers skim across the rivers. Skiers swish down the slopes. *(while)*

   While kayakers skim across the rivers, skiers swish down the

   slopes.

8. Vancouver Island is an excellent place to view killer whales. It is located on the Pacific coast. *(because)*

   Vancouver Island is an excellent place to view killer whales because it is

   located on the Pacific coast.

9. The tourists enjoyed a morning of whale watching. They visited the Parliament Building and had tea at the Empress Hotel. *(after)*

   After the tourists enjoyed a morning of whale watching, they visited

   the Parliament Building and had tea at the Empress Hotel.

Next Step Write a paragraph about a place you would like to visit. Use short, simple sentences in your paragraph. Read your paragraph aloud to a classmate. Then exchange your paragraph with him or her. Ask your classmate to revise your paragraph by combining the short sentences into complex sentences.

Writing Complex Sentences 2

Using adjective clauses to combine simple sentences will help you avoid unnecessary repetition in your writing. (Adjective clauses begin with words like *who, whose, which,* and *that.*) But be careful. Too many *who*'s or *which*'s will make your writing sound textbookish.

Who, whose, which, and **that** are called *relative pronouns.* See 706.3 in *Write Source* for a definition of relative pronouns and then write that definition below. (See page 517 and 746.1 for additional information.)

Definition: *A relative pronoun is both a . . .* pronoun and a connecting word. It

connects a dependent clause to an independent clause in a complex sentence.

Example

Shorter Sentences:

The ancient oak was destroyed in the storm. It stood near the park entrance.

Combined Sentence Using an Adjective Clause:

The ancient oak that stood at the park entrance **was destroyed in the storm.**
("That stood at the park entrance" is an adjective clause that modifies "oak.")

 Directions Combine each pair of simple sentences into one complex sentence using "who," "which," or "that" as a connector.

1. The bearded wrestler gave his opponent a bear hug. The bearded wrestler was slick with sweat.

   The bearded wrestler, who was slick with sweat, gave his opponent a

   bear hug.

2. The night air revived him after his day in the fields. The air was cool and sweet smelling.

   The night air, which was cool and sweet smelling, revived him after his

   day in the fields.

3. The construction workers were treated for heat exhaustion. They were building the new road through the park.

The construction workers who were building the new road through the

park were treated for heat exhaustion.

4. The sun is the center of our solar system. The sun is 93 million miles away.

The sun, which is 93 million miles away, is the center of our solar

system.

5. The tracks led to the old miner's shack. The tracks were freshly made.

The tracks, which were freshly made, led to the old miner's shack.

6. By the side of the road lay the ruined glider. It had been destined for Paris.

By the side of the road lay the ruined glider that had been destined

for Paris.

7. The agents escaped across the border. The agents set Mr. Goodwin free.

The agents who set Mr. Goodwin free escaped across the border.

8. Rudy seldom goes to the weight room. He would rather jog than lift weights.

Rudy, who would rather jog than lift weights, seldom goes to the

weight room.

Next Step Many of the complex sentences you have made require commas. (The commas set off the adjective clause from the rest of the sentence.) Read about **restrictive** and **nonrestrictive clauses** on pages 584–585 in *Write Source* and check your sentences. Read your sentences aloud to a partner.

Writing Complex Sentences 3

Adverb clauses are used to form complex sentences. They answer *how, when, where, why, how much,* or *under what condition.* Adverb clauses can be used at the beginning or at the end of complex sentences. Subordinating conjunctions—words like *after, although, before*—are used to introduce adverb clauses. (See pages 517 and 746.1 in *Write Source.*)

Example

Shorter Sentences:
John checked the apple for wormholes. He ate the apple.

Combined Sentences:
Before he ate the apple, **John checked it for wormholes.**
(An adverb clause at the beginning of a sentence needs a comma.)

John checked the apple for wormholes before he ate the apple.
(An adverb clause at the end of a sentence does not need a comma.)

 Combine each of the following sets of short sentences into one sentence using the subordinating conjunction listed in the parentheses. The first one has been done for you. *(Answers may vary.)*

1. I was about six years old. Something unforgettable happened. *(when)*

   When I was about six years old, something unforgettable happened.

2. Dad banged on my door. He yelled, "Get dressed and get downstairs!" *(as)*

   As Dad banged on my door, he yelled, "Get dressed and get downstairs!"

3. I realized I had forgotten my glasses. I was halfway down the stairs. *(before)*

   I was halfway down the stairs before I realized I had forgotten my glasses.

4. "What's wrong?" I asked. I struggled to pull on my shoes. *(while)*

"What's wrong?" I asked while I struggled to pull on my shoes.

5. My dad turned and yelled, "Fire!" He rushed out the front door. *(as)*

My dad turned and yelled, "Fire!" as he rushed out the front door.

6. He caught his breath. He said, "The neighbor's house is on fire!" *(when)*

When he caught his breath, he said, "The neighbor's house is on fire!"

7. My heart was beating wildly in my throat. I was still half asleep. *(although)*

Although I was still half asleep, my heart was beating wildly in my

throat.

8. I was hit by a blast of hot, smoky wind. I followed my dad outside. *(as)*

I was hit by a blast of hot, smoky wind as I followed my dad outside.

9. I was awake by then. I still hoped this was all a dream. *(although)*

Although I was awake by then, I still hoped this was all a dream.

Next Step Write a paragraph about fire. Maybe you have been involved in a fire. Maybe you have a relative who is a firefighter. Exchange your writing with a classmate. On your classmate's paper, look for ideas that might be combined using adverb clauses. Checkmark those ideas. When you get your paper back, try to combine the checkmarked ideas. Then read your revised paragraph to your classmate.

Writing Complex Sentences Review

Complex sentences are made up of an independent and a dependent clause. The independent clause in a complex sentence contains the most important idea in the sentence. The dependent clause contains a less important idea. The two clauses can be combined with a relative pronoun such as *who, whose, which,* or *that.* Clauses may also be combined with a subordinating conjunction such as *after, although, as, because, before, if, since, so, when, where, while, until, unless,* and so on.

Examples

Combining with a Relative Pronoun:
The writer is working on a new book. She has already published one book.
The writer, who has already published one book, is working on a new one.

Combining with a Subordinating Conjunction:
Carlos has started doing homework. He is getting better grades.
Since Carlos has started doing homework, he is getting better grades.

Note: When you are combining simple sentences into complex sentences, you may find it necessary to change an independent clause to a dependent clause. Examine the sentences carefully to see which clause is more important; then you'll know which clause (the less important one) can be subordinated.

 Directions Combine each of the following pairs of sentences into one complex sentence. Refer to pages 517 and 746 in *Write Source.*

(Answers may vary.)

1. The writer's first book wasn't very popular. She was not discouraged.

   Although the writer's first book wasn't very popular, she was not discouraged.

   _____

2. Yi had faith in her ability. She started a new book immediately.

   Because Yi had faith in her ability, she started a new book immediately.

   _____

3. The publisher suggested that Yi write a book on her experiences in gymnastics. She had been a successful gymnast.

   After Yi's success as a gymnast, the publisher suggested

   that she write a book on her experiences in gymnastics.

4. She thought the new book would be easy to write. It was on a topic familiar to her.

   Because the new book was on a topic familiar to her, she thought it

   would be easy to write.

5. Yi felt comfortable writing about gymnastics. She had been a gymnast since age three.

   Yi, who had been a gymnast since age three, felt comfortable writing

   about gymnastics.

6. Yi researched the topic. She discovered that gymnastics had changed considerably.

   As Yi researched the topic, she discovered that gymnastics had

   changed considerably.

7. Yi has been working hard on her new book. She has not worried about her first book.

   Since Yi has been working hard on her new book, she has not

   worried about her first book.

8. The publishers did not launch a nationwide promotional campaign immediately. They sensed outstanding sales potential.

   Although they sensed outstanding sales potential, the publishers did

   not launch a nationwide promotional campaign immediately.

Next Step Write a paragraph about an experience you had starting over after a first attempt failed. Then combine some of the sentences into complex sentences. Use a variety of dependent clauses. Make sure that the most important clause remains the independent clause.

Sentence Expanding

Successful writers have a knack for wording things the right way. They expand ideas with words and phrases that make their writing work. The smooth flow of their thoughts makes the actual words and sentences sound natural. (See pages 519–520 in *Write Source* for more examples.)

Details Added After the Basic Sentence:

He looks different, a little less like camp, a little more dressed up.

From *There's a Bat in Bunk Five* by Paula Danziger

Wil nodded to himself and slipped away, softly as a mouse, toward the back of the house where the tourists were never taken.

From "A Room Full of Leaves" by Joan Aiken

Details Added Before the Basic Sentence:

If his surroundings were gloomy and the company either boring to him or nonexistent, **he did not fidget.**

From "Total Stranger" by James Gould Cozzens

Details Added Before and After the Basic Sentence:

At the first sign of alarm, **he saw them clamber down the sapling and slip away** to the west beyond the gullberries.

From *The Yearling* by Marjorie Kinnan Rawlings

From then on, **it was like they were two dogs,** each waiting for the other one to make a move and start the fight.

From *Hoops* by Walter Dean Meyers

Directions   Study the sentences above. Read them out loud or have a partner read them to you. Listen carefully. Choose the two sentences you like best. On a separate piece of paper, write your own sentences, modeled after the professional writers' sentences. (To see how this is done, check out the example on pages 521–522 in *Write Source* under "Model Sentences.")

Directions Expand the three basic sentences that follow by adding a variety of details that will result in more meaningful thoughts.

(Answers will vary.)

1. Connie began to laugh.

In spite of the seriousness of the situation, Connie began to laugh, at first to

herself, then more and more loudly.

_____

_____

2. Charles turned quickly.

Anticipating the behind-the-back pass, Charles turned quickly to intercept it.

_____

_____

_____

3. Lakesha found the answer.

After hours of exhausting research in the library and on the Internet, Lakesha

found the answer to one of life's most perplexing problems.

_____

_____

Next Step Refer to one of the short stories you've read in class, an article in your favorite magazine, or a section in one of your favorite books and copy down two expanded sentences that you really like. Underline the basic sentence and circle the words, phrases, and clauses that were used to expand it. Compare your findings with those of a classmate.

Expanding Sentences with Phrases

Experienced writers often combine short, simple sentences into longer, more meaningful ones by using a phrase in one of the sentences. The following types of phrases are often the key when it comes to sentence combining: **prepositional, participial, infinitive, and appositive phrases.** (See pages 512, 519, 519 and 730.3–730.4 in *Write Source* to read about these phrases as you work on the sentences that follow.)

Examples

Infinitive Phrase:

I watched to see it land .
("To see it land" is an infinitive phrase.)

Prepositional Phrase:

I watched from my bedroom window .
("From my bedroom window" is a prepositional phrase.)

Appositive Phrase:

I watched from my bedroom window, a great viewing place .
("A great viewing place" is an appositive phrase renaming "window.")

Participial Phrase:

Wondering about the bird , **I watched from my bedroom window.**
("Wondering about the bird" is a participial phrase describing "I.")

Combined Sentence:

Wondering about the bird, I watched from my bedroom window, a great viewing place, to see it land.

 Directions Combine each pair of simple sentences using the type of phrase indicated in the parentheses. The first sentence has been done for you.

1. The movie is scary. It is showing at the Hargrove Theater. *(participial phrase)*

   The movie showing at the Hargrove Theater is scary.

2. Frank and Phil waited for their pizza. They are the famous Fettucini brothers. *(appositive phrase)*

Frank and Phil, the famous Fettucini brothers, waited for their pizza.

3. Glenna tore into a jelly-filled doughnut. It was from the "chewy and gooey" shelf in the bakery. *(prepositional phrase)*

Glenna tore into a jelly-filled doughnut from the "chewy and gooey"

shelf in the bakery.

4. Terrance studied each mountain bike. He wanted to determine which one would best meet his needs. *(infinitive phrase)*

Terrance studied each mountain bike to determine which one would

best meet his needs.

5. Alex blew a hole in one of his basketball shoes. He was running down the court. *(participial phrase)*

Running down the court, Alex blew a hole in one of his basketball

shoes.

6. Josie's hair can be uncontrollable. It is uncontrollable especially in wet weather. *("especially" + a prepositional phrase)*

Josie's hair can be uncontrollable, especially in wet weather.

7. The Blossoms played at the last school dance. They are music's answer to apple pie and sugar cookies. *(appositive phrase)*

The Blossoms, music's answer to apple pie and sugar cookies,

played at the last school dance.

Sentence Variety Review 1

Combining short, simple sentences into longer, more meaningful ones improves writing that otherwise sounds choppy. (See pages 511–522 in *Write Source* for more information.)

 Directions | Combine the following set of four short sentences into longer, smoother-reading ones. Follow the sentence "frames" when they are provided for you.

Shorter Sentences:

Juan likes to race on his BMX bike.

Juan will be competing in races this summer.

He is hoping to win 30 races.

Then he can try to win the state title.

Frame 1: Juan _____ *likes to race on his BMX* _____ bike,

therefore he _____ *will be competing in races this summer* _____

and hoping _____ *to win 30 races* _____ ,

so that _____ *he can then try to win the state title* _____ .

Frame 2: Juan, who _____ *races on his BMX bike* _____ ,

is hoping _____ *to win 30 races this summer* _____

so that _____ *he can then try to win the state title* _____ .

Frame 3: (Come up with your own version.)

_____

_____

_____

_____

Directions   Combine the following sets of simple sentences and then, on your own paper, finish the story. The first combined sentence has been done for you.

1. Jerri thought tryouts were easier last year. She was in sixth grade then.

Jerri thought tryouts were easier last year when she was in sixth grade.

2. She had thought for sure she had made the team. The coach had cut her.

She had thought for sure she had made the team, but the coach had

cut her.

3. She had wondered if Coach Anderson liked her. He sometimes yelled at her.

She had wondered if Coach Anderson liked her, because he sometimes

yelled at her.

4. Jerri now thinks something different. Maybe the coach was trying to help her.

Jerri now thinks that maybe the coach was trying to help her.

5. The practice lasted another 30 minutes. Coach Anderson stopped practice.

Coach Anderson stopped the practice after another 30 minutes.

6. He told the players to take a shower. He told them to check the board on their way out. A list of players who made the second cut would be posted.

He told them to take a shower and to check the board on their way

out for a list of players who made the second cut.

7. Jerri headed for the showers. She . . . (_Finish this story on your own paper._)

Next Step   Write a story about a situation that made you anxious. Exchange stories with a classmate. Check each other's work for choppiness. Correct or combine the sentences as necessary.

Sentence Variety Review 2

 Directions Use sentence-combining techniques to make each set of shorter sentences below into one longer sentence. Use the method indicated in parentheses at the end of each sentence to combine the sentences. Place your responses in the spaces provided. (For more information about sentence-combining techniques, see pages 511–514 in *Write Source*.)

1. Billy bowled three strikes. He bowled a split. *(Use a subordinating conjunction to make this a complex sentence.)*

   After Billy bowled three strikes, he bowled a split.

2. The match was long. The match was close. The match was exciting. *(Use a series of words.)*

   The match was long, close, and exciting.

3. Jess plays chess every day. Maria plays chess every day. *(Use a compound subject.)*

   Jess and Maria play chess every day.

4. I went to bed early. I couldn't fall asleep. *(Use a compound sentence.)*

   I went to bed early, but I couldn't fall asleep.

5. I always did my math homework. I still failed the exams. *(Use a compound verb.)*

   I always did my math homework and still failed the exams.

6. The officer asked us to move along. The officer smiled. *(Use the participle "smiling.")*

   The smiling officer asked us to move along.

Directions Combine each of the following sets of simple sentences into one complex sentence on the lines provided. The first sentence has been done for you.

1. Dan's right eye was twitching. He sat waiting for the test paper.

   Dan's right eye was twitching as he sat waiting for the test paper.

2. This was the last big English test of the term. Dan couldn't afford to fail it.

   Because this was the last big English test of the term, Dan couldn't

   afford to fail it.

3. Dan had studied hard for the test. He still didn't feel confident.

   Although Dan had studied hard for the test, he still didn't feel

   confident.

4. Five minutes passed. Mr. Adams looked down Dan's row. He saw Dan just sitting there.

   After five minutes passed, Mr. Adams looked down Dan's row and

   saw him just sitting there.

5. Dan couldn't write a single line. His mind was a complete blank.

   Dan couldn't write a single line because his mind was a complete blank.

6. Mr. Adams got up from his chair. He walked down the aisle toward Dan.

   After Mr. Adams got up from his chair, he walked down the aisle

   toward Dan.

Next Step Complete the story on your own paper. Be ready to read aloud in class your startling conclusion to "The Testing of Dan."

Parts of Speech
Activities

Every activity includes a main practice section in which you learn about or review the different parts of speech. Most of the activities include helpful *Write Source* references. In addition, the **Next Step** activities give you follow-up practice with certain skills.

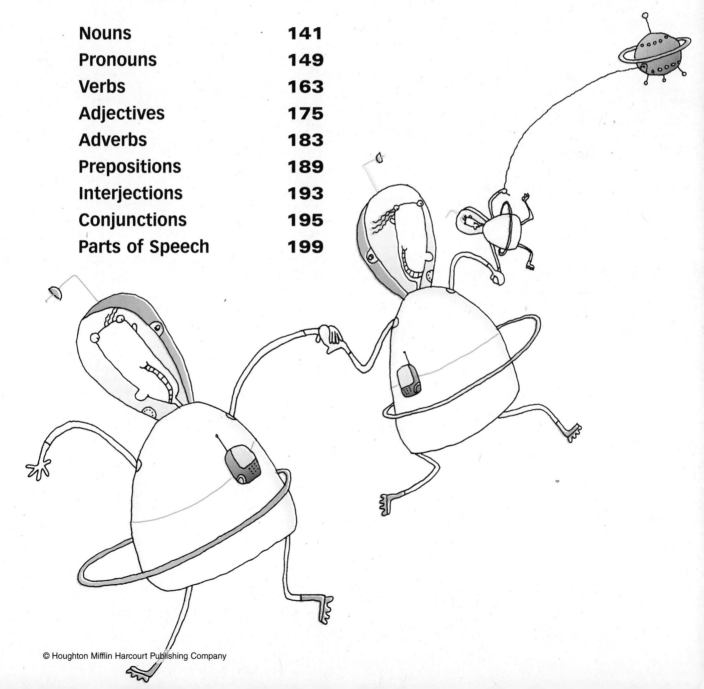

Common and Proper Nouns

A noun names a person, a place, a thing, or an idea. A **common noun** names any one of a group—not a specific person, place, thing, or idea. A common noun is *not* capitalized. A **proper noun** names a specific person, place, thing or idea. A proper noun is capitalized. (See 702.1 and 702.2 in *Write Source* for more information.)

Examples

Common Nouns	Proper Nouns
man	*José*
book	*American Heritage Dictionary*
city	*Baltimore*
team	*Chicago Cubs*

 Directions   Underline the nouns in the sentences that follow. Write "C" above each common noun and "P" above each proper noun. The first sentence has been done for you.

1. The words in our language have been put into eight groups called the parts of speech.

2. A noun is the part of speech that names a person, a place, a thing, or an idea.

3. Common nouns name common things: roads, cars, teams, and so on.

4. Proper nouns are more specific: Avery Road, Ford, and New York Yankees.

5. Can you pick the proper nouns out of this list: Saturn, meteor, rainbow, Apollo, John Glenn, Labor Day?

6. Remember, common nouns name common things and are not capitalized; proper nouns name specific things and are capitalized.

Directions Study the two lists of nouns that follow. Then add three nouns to each list. Make sure your nouns fit with the rest of the words in each list.
(Answers will vary.)

clock	**Big Ben**
book	*Gentle Ben*
car	**Volkswagen**
group	**Eagles**

_____   _____

_____   _____

_____   _____

Directions On the lines provided below, explain the difference between the nouns in the two lists above.
(Answers will vary.)

The nouns in the first list are common nouns—they do not name a specific

person, place, thing, or idea. The nouns in the second list are proper nouns—they

name a specific person, place, thing, or idea.

_____

_____

Note: Share your explanation with one of your classmates. Then compare it with the explanations in *Write Source* at 702.1 and 702.2. How close does your explanation match the ones in the book?

Next Step Select one noun from the first list at the top of this page (*clock* through *group*) as the beginning of a concrete poem or an acrostic poem. (See page 359 in *Write Source* for help with your poem.)

Concrete and Abstract Nouns

Ask my brother to wash dishes, and he'll answer, "Get real!" Actually, dirty dishes are "real" enough. You can see them, feel them—maybe even smell them! **Concrete nouns** name physical things like those dishes. But what if you can't see or touch something? Is love "real"? Of course it is. **Abstract nouns,** such as "love" and "poverty," name things that you can think about but can't see or touch. (See 702.3 and 702.4 in *Write Source*.)

Directions Underline all the words used as nouns in the sentences that follow. Then put a "C" above each concrete noun and an "A" above each abstract noun. Some words are tricky! They may name either a concrete or an abstract concept. The first sentence has been done for you.

1. When we gaze at <u>stars</u> (C), we are looking into the distant <u>past</u> (A), because the <u>light</u> (C) from <u>stars</u> (C) takes many <u>years</u> (A) to travel to <u>Earth</u> (C).

2. Some <u>dinosaurs</u> (C) half-buried their <u>eggs</u> (C) in <u>mud</u> (C), then covered the <u>tops</u> (C) with rotting <u>vegetation</u> (C) to warm them.

3. It is an amazing <u>fact</u> (A) that giant <u>redwoods</u> (C) transport <u>water</u> (C) tremendous <u>distances</u> (A) from their <u>roots</u> (C) to their <u>leaves</u> (C) without a <u>pump</u> (C).

4. By performing a <u>dance</u> (C), a <u>honeybee</u> (C) can tell other <u>workers</u> (C) in the <u>hive</u> (C) where <u>flowers</u> (C) filled with <u>nectar</u> (C) can be found.

5. <u>Hummingbirds</u> (C) are not shy; if you wear red <u>clothes</u> (C), they will fly close enough to get a careful <u>look</u> (A) at you.

6. The <u>Constitution</u> (C) guarantees all <u>Americans</u> (C) basic <u>freedoms</u> (A).

7. It was not easy for the original 13 <u>colonies</u> (C) to win those <u>freedoms</u> (A).

8. In fact, many <u>colonists</u> (C) did not like the <u>idea</u> (A) of a <u>rebellion</u> (A) against <u>England</u> (C).

9. Some continued to declare their loyalty to King George.
                                  A   C

10. The Eiffel Tower reminds me of drawings in my geometry book.

11. At the basketball game, one of the players had to leave the game because of an injury.

12. He sprained his ankle when he stepped on someone else's foot.

13. The teams showed good sportsmanship even when the spectators were a little rude.

14. Emilio went through a growth spurt last year.

15. Now his dream is to play football in high school.

Next Step Share the results of your work with a classmate. Discuss any differences you may find. Talk about ways you can distinguish between abstract and concrete nouns, and write your guidelines in the space below.

_____

_____

_____

Subject and Object Nouns

Every word in a sentence has a job to do. Nouns do more than just *name* a person, a place, a thing, or an idea. The specific job a noun does in a sentence depends on where it is used and how it is related to the other words. (See 704.4–704.7 in *Write Source*.)

Examples

Subject Noun:
Our family loved spending afternoons in the park.
(A *subject noun* names the person, place, thing, or idea that is doing the action or is being talked about: "family" is a subject noun.)

Predicate Noun:
Our favorite game was football.
(A *predicate noun* follows a linking verb or a form of the *be* verb—*is, are, was, were*—and repeats or renames the subject: "football" renames *game.)*

Possessive Noun:
My family's favorite lunch was pizza.
(A *possessive noun* is a noun that shows ownership: "family's" is a possessive noun.)

Object Noun:
We would often eat our lunch there.
(A noun becomes an *object noun* when it is used as the direct object, indirect object, or object of the preposition: "lunch" is a direct object.)

 Directions Label each underlined noun in the following sentences. Use "SN" for subject noun, "PN" for predicate noun, "POS" for possessive noun, "ON" for object noun. The first two sentences have been done for you.

SN **1.** The small <u>park</u> in my neighborhood used to be my favorite place.

ON **2.** My mother took me to the <u>park</u> almost every day.

ON **3.** I chased <u>squirrels</u> and <u>pigeons</u> around the huge trees.

ON **4.** My mother gave me <u>ice cream</u> and other treats.

POS **5.** Kids from all over the <u>city's</u> south side gathered in the park.

SN   **6.** Parents sat and talked on benches while the <u>kids</u> played on the equipment.

ON   **7.** Old people came and played <u>chess</u> and checkers on stone tables in the sun.

SN   **8.** City police <u>officers</u> patrolled the park on their bicycles.

PN   **9.** The police officers were <u>part</u> of the fun.

ON   **10.** One police officer even gave me an ice-cream <u>cone</u>.

SN   **11.** Last summer many city <u>workers</u> went on strike.

PN   **12.** In just a few days, the park was a total <u>disaster</u>.

ON   **13.** People discarded <u>paper</u> and litter on the grass and playground.

SN   **14.** <u>Parents</u> didn't want their kids playing in a bunch of garbage.

POS   **15.** The park had been a green oasis in the <u>city's</u> concrete desert.

ON   **16.** Neighborhood residents organized a clean-up-the-park <u>campaign</u>.

SN   **17.** On the designated day, practically the whole <u>neighborhood</u> showed up for work.

ON   **18.** People swept, raked, and picked up all the <u>garbage</u> in the park.

POS   **19.** Four ladies from our building planted flowers along the <u>park's</u> walkway.

PN   **20.** The park was once again a wonderful <u>place</u> for everyone to enjoy.

Next Step Write a paragraph describing a time when people joined together to accomplish something. It might be a neighborhood project or something done in school. Where the activity took place doesn't really matter. What matters is that you describe something that people thought needed to be done and got together to do. You might even want to write about something that you did with members of your own family.

Specific Nouns

Specific nouns are especially helpful when you are trying to create a clear image or word picture for a reader. Notice the difference between the two example sentences below. The first sentence contains general nouns, and it doesn't express a very clear idea. The second sentence, which includes more specific nouns, does express a clear idea. (See page 471 in *Write Source* for more information.)

The **scientist wanted to study** animals **in another** country. (general nouns)

Jane Goodall **wanted to study** chimpanzees **in** Tanzania. (specific nouns)

Look at the examples below. Notice that the nouns move from very general at the top to very specific at the bottom. By using a good number of specific nouns in your writing, you will make it easier for the reader to understand exactly what you are saying.

Examples

person	place	thing	idea
man	building	book	pain
artist	arena	reference book	headache
Vincent van Gogh	Madison Square Garden	Farmers' Almanac	migraine

 Directions Now think of three nouns for each of the categories below. Each noun you add must be more specific than the one before it, as in the examples above. *(Answers will vary.)*

person	place	thing	idea

Example

    The <u>car</u> drove past the <u>building</u>.

a. _The foreign car drove past the government building._

b. _The Toyota convertible drove past the White House._

Directions Revise each of the following sentences twice. Make sentence B even more specific than sentence A. (Add or change other words as necessary to create a better sentence.) *(Answers will vary.)*

1. The **animal** is in the **building**.

a. _The dog is in the kennel._

b. _The German shepherd is in Brownsville Animal Shelter._

2. The **doctor** performed the **operation**.

a. _The specialist performed the heart surgery._

b. _The cardiologist performed the bypass surgery._

3. The **singer** was given an **award**.

a. _The pop singer was given a trophy._

b. _Celine Dion was given a Grammy._

4. A **relative** came down with an **illness**.

a. _My sister came down with the measles._

b. _My sister Joan came down with the German measles._

5. The **dog** ran around the **tree**.

a. _The terrier ran around the oak tree._

b. _The Irish terrier ran around the dead oak tree._

Pronouns and Antecedents

You always want to write so your readers clearly understand what it is you're trying to say. You also must make sure that the antecedent of a pronoun (the word the pronoun refers to) is clear in your writing. (For more information, see 706.1 in *Write Source*.)

Example

Unclear Pronoun Use:

I took my car to the corner gas station because it was nearly empty.
(This sentence does not clearly state *what* was nearly empty—the car or the gas station—because the antecedent of the pronoun "it" is unclear.)

Clear Pronoun and Antecedent:

Because my car was nearly empty, I took it to the corner gas station.
("Car" is definitely the antecedent of the pronoun "it" in this sentence.)

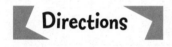 **Directions** Rewrite each of the following sentences so that the pronoun has a clearly stated antecedent. Be sure to use the boldfaced pronoun in your new sentence. The first sentence has been done for you.

(Answers may vary.)

1. Reggie sat in the first row of the theater since **it** was empty.

   Since the first row of the theater was empty, Reggie sat in it.

2. When I put my foot into the shoe, **it** was wet.

   My foot was wet when I put it into the shoe.

3. When the ice floe reached the old dam, **it** broke.

   The ice floe broke when it reached the old dam.

4. After he'd left the present on the doorstep, Gerard realized **it** was the wrong one.

   Gerald realized it was the wrong present after he'd left it on the doorstep.

5. Though the chauffeur drove the limousine into the fence, **it** wasn't damaged.

   The limousine wasn't damaged even though the chauffeur drove it into the

   fence.

6. I can't give the bone to my dog because **it** is too sharp.

   Because the bone is too sharp, I can't give it to my dog.

7. I don't go to movies with my young cousins because **they** are too violent. (*they* becomes *them*)

   Because movies are too violent, I don't go to them with my young

   cousins.

8. Traffic, on the way to my aunt's dinner, **which** was terrible, made us late.

   Traffic, which was terrible on the way to my aunt's dinner, made us late.

Next Step Turn to page 714 in *Write Source* to find a chart of singular and plural personal pronouns. Write at least three sentences that use a pronoun with its antecedent. Draw an arrow from the pronoun to its antecedent.

Types of Pronouns 1

Pronouns do a great job of standing in for nouns. But some pronouns do more: *Reflexive* and *intensive* pronouns, for example, give their antecedents extra emphasis.

Another group of pronouns—*indefinite pronouns*—also stand in for nouns, but they don't refer to a definite person or thing. Indefinite pronouns are often used without antecedents. Indefinite pronouns keep the subject vague—which might be a relief to the person who is the subject: *Somebody* spilled the cereal. *Nobody* cleaned it up. *Somebody* left the bike in the driveway. (See 708.2, 708.3, and 710.1 in *Write Source* for more information.)

Examples

Reflexive Pronoun:

Little Jeff has finally learned how to dress himself.
(The reflexive pronoun "himself" throws the action back on the subject of the sentence. The sentence would not be complete without it.)

Intensive Pronoun:

Little Jeff himself **put on his pants**.
(The intensive pronoun "himself" intensifies or emphasizes its antecedent. However, it's not necessary; the sentence is complete without it.)

Indefinite Pronoun:

Somebody **left these pants on the floor.**
(The indefinite pronoun "somebody" doesn't stand in for a particular person. The person is indefinite or unknown.)

> **Directions** Write a reflexive, intensive, or indefinite pronoun in the blanks in the sentences below. Write "Ref" above each reflexive pronoun, "Int" above each intensive pronoun, and "Ind" above each indefinite pronoun. The first sentence has been done for you.

1. _____*Something*_____ warned me not to make a sound as I tiptoed up the

   dark staircase.

2. Instead, I ended up making loud creaking sounds as if King Kong

   _____*himself*_____ were stomping up to the second story.

3. I could not stop _____ *Ref* **myself** _____ from trembling like a leaf.

4. As I reached the top of the stairs, I felt _____ *Ind* **something** _____ brush my

leg, and then I heard it throw _____ *Ref* **itself** _____ down the stairs.

5. I stood as if frozen to the landing, desperately telling _____ *Ref* **myself** _____

to calm down.

6. As my eyes adjusted to the darkness, I looked around for _____ *Ind* **something** _____

to hide behind.

7. Just then, I saw _____ *Ind* **something** _____ with many shining eyes watching

me from under the bed.

8. I threw _____ *Ref* **myself** _____ in the direction of the light switch.

9. I flipped the switch and found _____ *Ref* **myself** _____ face-to-face with a

possum and her brood.

10. _____ *Ind* **Nothing** _____ could have prepared me for what I saw next: the

possum family suddenly appeared to be dead.

11. Thinking of _____ *Ref* **myself** _____ as a murderer, I carried the throw rug

full of "dead" possums out to the garden.

12. Later, when I took Mom out to the garden, _____ *Ind* **nothing** _____—not

one possum—was there.

13. Much later I realized that _____ *Ind* **no one** _____ had ever told me what

"playing possum" really meant.

Next Step Write a short story about a scary experience you actually had or about a scary experience someone told you about. Try to use at least one reflexive pronoun, one intensive pronoun, and one indefinite pronoun in your story. Exchange papers with a friend. Enjoy the story and then check to see if the pronouns have been used correctly.

Types of Pronouns 2

Review the special types of pronouns listed below. Notice how each type functions. It might be to ask a question, to point out something, or to relate a subordinate clause to a main clause. (See 706.3, 706.4, and 708.1 in *Write Source* for more information.)

Examples

Relative Pronouns:

Wolves are not just wild dogs that <u>can be tamed</u>.
("That" refers back to "dogs" and links the underlined subordinate clause to the main clause of the sentence.)

Interrogative Pronouns:

To whom did you give your locker combination?
(An interrogative pronoun asks a question. Use "who," "whose," or "whom" when asking questions about people. Use "which" and "what" when asking about things or ideas.)

Demonstrative Pronouns:

These seeds will sprout, but those are old and rotten.
(A demonstrative pronoun points out a thing or an idea without naming it.)
Note: It is incorrect to pair demonstrative pronouns with "here" or "there," such as "This here book . . . ".

> **Directions**   Write a pronoun in the blank in each sentence below. Write "I" above interrogative pronouns, "D" above demonstrative pronouns, and "R" above relative pronouns. The first sentence has been done for you.

(Answers will vary.)

1. The sky filled with an eerie glow, ____*which*____ we suddenly realized was fire!
   <small>R</small>

2. The mall parking lot was full of snowy mounds, ____*which*____ only an
   <small>R</small>

   hour before had been cars of many shapes and colors.

3. The contractor knows how to select paint _____*that*_____ will be durable
   <small>R</small>

   under wet or moist conditions.

4. _____*This/That*_____ is a mountain pass that an experienced climber could make,
   <small>D</small>

   but _____*that/this*_____ is a deadly crevasse no one could get through.
   <small>D</small>

5. After its 40-foot columns rotted, a 200-year-old building at Oxford

University was saved because its original builder, planning ahead, had

planted an oak grove _____*that*_____ provided the replacement columns.
<small>R</small>

6. _____*What*_____ word game would you like to play?
<small>I</small>

7. Stepping into the jungle _____*that*_____ grew in a thick, thorny tangle,
<small>R</small>

the inexperienced explorer was instantly lost.

8. _____*That/This*_____ animal is a crocodile, and _____*this/that*_____ is an
<small>D</small> <small>D</small>

alligator.

9. If you had to list the 10 most important inventions of the twentieth century,

_____*what*_____ would they be?
<small>I</small>

10. The field, _____*which*_____ was still wet from yesterday's rain, turned into
<small>R</small>

a muddy mess by halftime.

11. Mr. Lawrence, _____*whom*_____ the students secretly nicknamed Lumpy,
<small>R</small>

was known for his huge midafternoon snacks.

12. _____*These/Those*_____ cotton jerseys are comfortable, but _____*those/these*_____
<small>D</small> <small>D</small>

wool ones are scratchy.

13. The coach, _____*whose*_____ job hinged on winning the last two games of
<small>R</small>

the season, looked very nervous.

14. _____*Which*_____ country produces more oil, Mexico or Venezuela?
<small>I</small>

Next Step Write a paragraph about a sports competition you recently participated in or watched. Check to make sure you have used relative pronouns correctly. When you have finished your paragraphs, read them aloud to a classmate.

Person and Number of a Pronoun

The **person** of a pronoun tells whether a pronoun is the speaker in a sentence (first person=*I, we,* and so on), the person being spoken to (second person=*you*), or the person or thing being talked about (third person=*he, it, they,* and so on).

The **number** of a pronoun tells whether a pronoun is singular or plural. The number of a pronoun and its antecedent must match. (See 706.1 and 712.1–712.4 in *Write Source.*)

Examples

Singular Pronoun:
A <u>monarch butterfly</u> must spend its winter in a warm climate.

Plural Pronoun:
In late August, <u>monarch butterflies</u> begin their southern migration.

 Directions Write the pronoun that completes each sentence below. The first sentence has been done for you.

1. When fall flowers bloom, _____*they*_____ signal the monarch migration.
(it, they)

2. An organization called Monarch Watch involves thousands of volunteers in

_____*its*_____ tagging and logging of the butterflies.
(its, their)

3. The volunteers gently capture the monarchs and tag _____*them*_____.
(it, them)

4. They fill in data sheets and send _____*them*_____ to research centers.
(it, them)

5. _____*She*_____ would like to be a Monarch Watch volunteer some day.
(Her, She)

6. Environmentalists want to know whether monarchs follow a path or simply

travel in a particular direction as _____*they*_____ move across the continent.
(it, they)

7. _____They_____ hope to see if the migration is the same from year to year.
(They, You)

8. Monarch Watch volunteers are often teachers and students who conduct

research as part of _____their_____ science classes.
(their, our)

9. Using a good butterfly net, a student captures _____his or her_____ butterfly,
(his or her, their)

then holds _____it_____ gently while applying a self-sticking tag.
(them, it)

10. A butterfly is tagged on a cell under _____its_____ hind wing.
(his, its)

11. The mitten-shaped cell is near a butterfly's center of gravity, where the

sticker application doesn't restrict _____its_____ flight.
(their, its)

12. Before each butterfly is released, _____its_____ tag number and other
(their, its)

information are recorded.

13. Second graders are some of the best taggers, because _____they_____ can
(they, he)

apply the self-sticking tags with _____their_____ smaller fingertips!
(their, his)

14. The more kids know about butterflies, the better _____they_____ will
(we, they)

understand the connections among all living things.

15. Eastern monarchs travel to forest sites in central Mexico, where 40 million

of _____them_____ roost at a site that's open to the public.
(they, them)

16. _____You_____ can see western monarchs in smaller, temporary sites from
(You, They)

Mendocino, California, to the Ensenada region of Baja California Sur.

Uses of Pronouns

Just like the nouns they replace, pronouns can be subjects or objects in a sentence. Possessive pronouns can also stand in for possessive nouns. Most of the time, using the correct form of the pronoun isn't a problem. But sometimes, substituting a pronoun for a noun can result in confusion.

As you review the examples below, you'll notice that many problems with pronouns happen because people write the way they talk. (See 710.1 and 714.2 in *Write Source* for more information.)

Examples

Incorrect:

Everyone has their own ticket.
("Their" is plural and does not match its singular antecedent, "everyone.")

Correct:

Everyone has his or her own ticket.
("His or her" is singular. It now matches its singular antecedent, "everyone.")
Note: When it's not clear if the pronoun should be male or female, use the phrase "his or her."

Incorrect:

When Joan and Sharone were neighbors, she souped up her BMX bike.

Correct:

When Joan was Sharone's neighbor, she souped up Sharone's BMX bike.

Incorrect:

If someone sprains a knee, you will need physical therapy.
("Someone" is a third-person subject. "You" is a second-person subject. The pronouns need to be in the same person or else it is not clear whose knee is sprained.)

Correct:

If someone sprains a knee, he or she will need physical therapy.

Incorrect:

John he makes great chili.
(Avoid using a pronoun immediately following a noun.)

Correct:

John makes great chili.

> **Directions** — Correct the common pronoun errors in the sentences below by rewriting the sentences in the spaces provided. Be prepared to discuss why you made the corrections. The first sentence has been done for you.

1. Sue's dog, Voltaire, he likes to play soccer, but they often play too rough.

   Sue's dog, Voltaire, likes to play soccer, but he often plays too rough.

2. I don't suppose you thought about a person's feelings when you took my sweater and stretched it out, and then gave it back to that person without having it cleaned.

   I don't suppose you thought about my feelings when you took my sweater and

   stretched it out, and then gave it back to me without having it cleaned.

   _____

3. Soon, if an athlete injures their knee, doctors will be able to repair the sinews with a synthetic material that is twice as strong as their original muscle.

   Soon, if an athlete injures his or her knee, doctors will be able to repair the

   sinews with a synthetic material that is twice as strong as his or her original

   muscle.

4. If a student wants to participate in extracurricular sports, you have to maintain a passing grade point average.

   If a student wants to participate in extracurricular sports, he or she has to

   maintain a passing grade point average.

Next Step In one of the books you are reading, find a paragraph that uses a number of pronouns. Then list the pronouns on a sheet of paper and identify each one as either (1) a subject pronoun, (2) an object pronoun, or (3) a possessive pronoun. If you find an odd use that doesn't seem to fit the basic rules, ask your teacher for help.

Pronoun-Antecedent Agreement 1

One of the most important rules of writing is this one: *A pronoun must agree with its antecedent.*

Here's what the rule means: Every time you use a pronoun in place of a noun, you must be sure that the pronoun is the same number (singular or plural) and the same person (first, second, third) as the original noun. (For more information, see 706.1 in *Write Source.*)

Example

The four deer scattered as the skunk approached them.

(A pronoun must agree in number with its antecedent. Because the noun "deer" is plural, the pronoun "them" must also be plural.)

 Directions   Cross out the incorrect pronouns in the following sentences. Write corrections above them. The first one has been done for you.

1. My grandma rolled her eyes when she heard ~~they~~ *she* can buy eggs laid by

   vegetarian chickens that don't eat bugs or meat by-products.

2. Grandma always thought having chickens eat bugs was good for ~~it~~ *them*.

3. Grandma says that when she was growing up, kids were expected to eat

   whatever was put in front of ~~you~~ *them*, and so were chickens.

4. "Things change," I said. "When IBM started in the '50s, ~~he~~ *it* thought five

   computers throughout the world would be enough to do the job."

5. My grandma said ~~her~~ *she* doesn't see what computers have to do with chickens.

6. I pointed out that computers are used to coordinate the shipping of fruits and

   vegetables, making ~~it~~ *them* available throughout the world any time of the year.

7. Grandma said we should ask a chicken if ~~they like~~ *it likes* fruits and vegetables

   before we make ~~them~~ *it* eat this food.

8. "Not chickens, Grandma—people demand special eggs, because ~~he's~~ *they've* gotten

   used to foods from all over the world," I explained.

9. My grandma says ~~they know~~ *she knows* what ~~they~~ *she* would do if somebody started

   demanding special eggs at ~~their~~ *her* house.

10. Grandma would plunk that peanut butter jar down on the table and invite

    her guest to make ~~themself~~ *himself or herself* a sandwich.

11. "What if a person eats a special diet for ~~their~~ *his or her* health?" I asked.

12. As long as she doesn't have to cook it, Grandma supposes a person can eat

    whatever he or she wants.

13. A person should mind ~~their~~ *his or her* manners, Grandma says.

14. A guest should eat what ~~they're~~ *he or she is* served.

15. People shouldn't make unreasonable demands on the hostess even if it's

    important to stay on ~~her~~ *their* diets.

16. People should thank the cook, Grandma says, even if ~~him~~ *their* meal is terrible!

Next Step Write a story about something your grandmother or grandfather says (or base your story on a fictional grandmother or grandfather). Try to use a few pronouns in your story. Underline your pronouns and circle their antecedents. Check that the pronouns agree in number and in person with their antecedents. Share your story aloud with a partner.

Pronoun-Antecedent Agreement 2

Do you sometimes need an "antecedent detector"? You will need to develop your own sense of what makes pronouns and their antecedents clear and easy to read. Rewriting poorly written sentences—like the ones below—will help you develop this sense and, in turn, help you become a better writer. (For more information, see 706.1 and 706.3 in *Write Source*.)

Example

Confusing Pronoun Reference:

As I dug into my meal, Karen stuck her gum on my plate, <u>which</u> tasted as good at it looked.

Corrected Sentence:

As Karen stuck her gum on my plate, I dug into my meal, <u>which</u> tasted as good as it looked.

 Directions Find the confusing pronoun references in the sentences below. Then, rewrite each sentence on the lines below it. The first sentence has been done for you. *(Answers will vary.)*

1. Most kids appreciate a practical joke, especially if they are a little bit crazy.

   Most kids appreciate a practical joke, especially if it is a little bit crazy.

2. Jack's dad took us for ice cream after the game, while he was bragging about how he made the three-point shot that won the game.

   While Jack was bragging about how he made the three-point shot that won the

   game, his dad took us for ice cream.

3. As I looked out the bedroom window, a doe ran behind our truck, but it moved before I could grab my camera.

As I looked out the bedroom window, a doe ran behind our truck, but

she moved before I could grab my camera.

4. At sunrise in the mountains, the campers were able to ignore their aching muscles and sore feet because they were so beautiful.

Because the mountains were so beautiful at sunrise, the campers

were able to ignore their aching muscles and sore feet.

5. The Scouts had been hiking so long in the mountains that they were worn down.

The Scouts were worn down after they had been hiking so long in the

mountains.

6. Lots of buses stop in front of the school to pick up students, all of them smelling like diesel fuel.

Lots of buses, all of them smelling like diesel fuel, stop in front of the school

to pick up students.

7. I picked up some pretzels when I went for a walk with my dogs, and I ate them.

When I went for a walk with my dogs, I picked up some pretzels, and I ate them.

8. I helped dry towels with my sisters, by hanging them on the clothesline.

I helped my sisters dry towels, by hanging them on the clothesline.

Next Step Write down a verse from a song—a traditional song or a song you've heard on the radio. Circle the pronouns. Draw a line from each pronoun to its antecedent. Are all the antecedents clear?

Action, Linking, and Helping Verbs

I'd saved up for months for my trip to the Super Bowl. The game electrified the crowd. My favorite team won in overtime. But when a reporter asked me what I thought of the game, I could think of only one word: "Awesome!" A few vivid action verbs that afternoon would have saved my big TV moment. Action verbs can also save your writing, turning it from dull to exciting. (See page 718 in *Write Source* for more information.)

Examples

Linking Verbs:

You <u>could be</u> **a radio programmer and broadcaster.**

Action Verbs:

You <u>could create</u> **and** <u>broadcast</u> **your own radio program.**

(In this sentence, "could" is a helping verb.)

 Directions Underline the verbs twice in each of the following sentences. (Don't forget to underline helping verbs as well.) Label each action verb with an "A" and each linking verb with an "L." The first sentence has been done for you.

1. Some recent movies and television shows <u>dramatize</u> *A* the danger of asteroids to life on Earth.

2. Some scientists <u>feel</u> *L* that at least one huge asteroid <u>smashed</u> *A* into Earth during the time that dinosaurs <u>roamed</u> *A* the planet.

3. Under the ocean near Mexico's Yucatan Peninsula <u>lies</u> *A* an impact crater nearly 180 kilometers wide.

4. Scientists believe *(A)* an asteroid crashed *(A)* there 65 million years ago and raised *(A)* a cloud of dust and ash that cooled *(A)* Earth and killed *(A)* the dinosaurs.

5. While another asteroid strike like that might not destroy *(A)* the human race, it could wreck *(A)* our civilization.

6. Asteroids orbit *(A)* the sun in a "belt" between Mars and Jupiter.

7. Sometimes the gravity of those planets nudges *(A)* an asteroid out of the belt, and it crosses *(A)* Earth's orbit.

8. Normally Earth's gravity then swings *(A)* the asteroid farther toward the sun, where it disintegrates *(A)*.

9. Earth has *(L)* several large craters, however, where asteroids have struck *(A)* in the past.

10. Because the moon has *(L)* no atmosphere, impact craters actually cover *(A)* its surface.

11. Most asteroid strikes happened *(A)* long, long ago, during the fury of the solar system's formation.

12. In fact, the chance that a major asteroid will strike *(A)* Earth is *(L)* very, very small.

13. Still, a number of government agencies watch *(A)* the skies for "killer" asteroids.

14. Even though the chance of a deadly strike is *(L)* slim, "Better safe than sorry."

Next Step Write a paragraph describing an event you witnessed: a concert, a parade, a game. Use action verbs to make your paragraphs come to life for the reader. Share your paragraph with a partner.

Simple Verb Tenses

A verb does more than express an action or link the subject to another word in a sentence. A verb also expresses tense, or time. A good place to begin a study of verb tenses is with the three simple tenses: **present, past,** and **future.** (See page 720 in *Write Source* for more information.)

Examples

Present Tense:

John <u>walks</u> up to me, his backpack dragging on the ground.

Past Tense:

John <u>walked</u> up to me, his backpack dragging on the ground.

Future Tense:

John <u>will walk</u> up to me, his backpack dragging on the ground.

 Directions Underline the verb twice in each of the following sentences. Then put each sentence in a different "time zone." That is, rewrite each sentence twice, using the verb in all three simple tenses. (Also, underline the verbs with two lines in your new sentences.) The first one has been done for you.

1. **Present:** *My battery-driven car <u>bumps</u> into the furniture.*

   Past: *My battery-driven car <u>bumped</u> into the furniture.*

   Future: *My battery-driven car <u>will bump</u> into the furniture.*

   _____

2. **Present:** *I <u>call</u> the folks at the AAA auto club to help me.*

   _____

   Past: *I <u>called</u> the folks at the AAA auto club to help me.*

   Future: *I <u>will call</u> the folks at the AAA auto club to help me.*

   _____

3. **Present:** In two minutes flat, the person from AAA starts my car.

Past: In two minutes flat, the person from AAA started my car.

Future: In two minutes flat, the person from AAA will start my car.

4. **Present:** Mikey balances two dozen paperbacks on his head at once.

Past: Mikey balanced two dozen paperbacks on his head at once.

Future: Mikey will balance two dozen paperbacks on his head at once.

5. **Present:** The books slide off in all directions.

Past: The books slid off in all directions.

Future: The books will slide off in all directions.

6. **Present:** The class laughs uproariously.

Past: The class laughed uproariously.

Future: The class will laugh uproariously.

Next Step Write one sentence about your last summer. Now put it in present and future tenses. Write one sentence about your next summer. Then rewrite it in past and present tenses.

Irregular Verbs

The principal parts of a verb are the **present tense,** the **past tense,** and the **past participle.** While the past principal parts of most verbs are created simply by adding "ed" to the main verb (*like, liked, liked*), the different parts of irregular verbs follow no set pattern (*run, ran, run; bite, bit, bitten*). This makes it more challenging to use the principal parts correctly in your writing. The following activity can help. (See page 722 in *Texas Write Source* for a chart of irregular verbs.)

 Directions   A good way to learn these irregular verbs is simply to say them over to yourself several times. They have a certain rhythm that helps to make them stick in your mind. Try these easier ones first. Look at them and say them to yourself several times.

Present Tense	Past Tense	Past Participle
begin	began	begun
bite	bit	bitten
drink	drank	drunk
see	saw	seen
write	wrote	written

Of course, there are many more troublesome verbs, including the following:

bring	brought	brought
burst	burst	burst
drown	drowned	drowned
swing	swung	swung
wake	woke	woken

 Directions   Now try to fill in the blanks below with the principal parts of the verbs you just studied. Try to do it without looking!

begin	began	begun
drink	drank	drunk
write	wrote	written
swing	swung	swung
drown	drowned	drowned

Directions Now turn to the chart of irregular verbs on page 722 in *Write Source*. Read it slowly to yourself. Listen as a classmate reads it to you. Make note of the verbs that cause you trouble. Study those. Then close your book and fill in the chart that follows. (Check your work when you finish.)

Present Tense	Past Tense	Past Participle
am, be	was, were	been
bite	bit	bitten
bring	brought	brought
catch	caught	caught
come	came	come
do	did	done
draw	drew	drawn
eat	ate	eaten
fall	fell	fallen
fight	fought	fought
fly	flew	flown
know	knew	known
lie (recline)	lay	lain
set	set	set
shake	shook	shaken
swim	swam	swum

Next Step Use the most troublesome verbs (from the list above) in a paragraph. Here's a possible starting point:

I brought a water balloon to the picnic, and it . . .

Perfect Tenses

At times, the action you want to express isn't clearly a present, past, or future action. For example, let's say that you began cleaning your messy locker five days ago and you are still cleaning it. Your cleaning is neither a past action nor a present action. Instead, it is an ongoing action. In this type of situation, you need to use one of the three perfect tenses to state the action. Note the use of the perfect tenses in the following sentences. The verb in each sentence is in color. (See 724.1–724.3 in *Write Source* for more examples.)

Examples

Present Perfect Tense:
The amusement park has remained **my favorite place to spend a summer day.**

Past Perfect Tense:
Before this year, the Monster ride had frightened **me.**

Future Perfect Tense:
After this summer, I will have visited **the park for six straight years.**

Directions Using *Write Source*, answer the following questions about the perfect tenses.

1. A verb in the *present perfect tense* expresses action that __began in the past__ __but continues or is completed in the present.__ _____

2. A verb in the *past perfect tense* expresses action that __began in the past and__ __was completed in the past.__ _____

3. A verb in the *future perfect tense* expresses action that __will begin in the__ __future and will be completed by a specific time in the future.__

Directions Underline the verb twice in each of these sentences. Don't forget to underline helping verbs as well. In the space provided, label each verb as "present perfect," "past perfect," or "future perfect." The first one has been done for you.

present perfect **1.** Ned Frap, the ruler of the planet, has escaped in a spacepod.

past perfect **2.** An earthquake had leveled his plastic dome.

future perfect **3.** He will have used all his energy pellets before nightfall.

past perfect **4.** Ned had lived in his dome for six years.

past perfect **5.** In those six years, he had never gone outside.

Directions Underline the verb twice in each of the following sentences. Then rewrite each sentence by changing the verb to the tense indicated in parentheses. Remember that all perfect tenses are composed of a form of *have* plus the past participle of the main verb. The first one has been done for you.

1. The Phantom Blur prepares very carefully for the mission. *(present perfect)*

The Phantom Blur has prepared very carefully for the mission.

2. He sneaks into embassies, castles, and prisons. *(present perfect)*

He has sneaked into embassies, castles, and prisons.

3. Tomorrow, the Phantom Blur will attempt a new mission. *(future perfect)*

Tomorrow, the Phantom Blur will have attempted a new mission.

4. At first, he considered the mission a pushover. *(past perfect)*

At first, he had considered the mission a pushover.

5. Perhaps by tomorrow night he will change his mind. *(future perfect)*

Perhaps by tomorrow night he will have changed his mind.

Next Step Write your own science fiction story in several paragraphs. Use present perfect, past perfect, and future perfect tenses at least two times each in your story and underline each verb and helping verb. Share your finished story with the class by reading it aloud. Have students identify the verbs and their tenses.

Transitive and Intransitive Verbs

There are two types of action verbs—transitive and intransitive. **Transitive** verbs "transfer" their action to a direct object (and sometimes to an indirect object). The direct object completes the meaning of the sentence, as in the examples that follow. An **intransitive** verb completes its meaning without an object. (See 728.2, 728.3, and 730.1 in *Write Source* for more information.)

Examples

Transitive Verb:

The teacher handed me the extinguisher.

A **direct object** receives the direct action of the verb. It answers the question *who* or *what* after the verb. The teacher handed me what? ("extinguisher"— direct object)

An **indirect object** is indirectly affected by the verb. It tells *to whom* or *for whom* something is done. The teacher handed the extinguisher to whom? ("me"—indirect object)

Intransitive Verb:

Everyone in our class walked quietly down the hall.

An intransitive verb does not need to transfer its action to a direct object to complete the thought. In this sentence, the verb "walked" is intransitive and does not have a direct object.

 Directions Write "T" in front of sentences with transitive verbs and "I" in front of sentences with intransitive verbs. Underline each verb twice; for each transitive verb, circle the direct object. The first one has been done for you.

_____T_____ **1.** Students sometimes <u>set off</u> fire (alarms) by accident.

_____I_____ **2.** Yesterday's alarm <u>rang</u> for five minutes.

_____T_____ **3.** The principal <u>gave</u> specific (instructions) over the P.A.

_____T_____ **4.** Students and teachers <u>placed</u> their (books) on their desks.

_____T_____ **5.** Teachers hurriedly ushered (students) into the hall.

_____T_____ **6.** They counted the (students) as they left the classroom.

_____I_____ **7.** Out in the hall, smoke poured from the ductwork.

_____I_____ **8.** Surprisingly, nobody panicked.

_____T_____ **9.** The students followed (directions) carefully.

_____I_____ **10.** They filed out to their designated areas.

_____T_____ **11.** Students had learned good (habits) from previous fire drills.

_____I_____ **12.** The fire was burning in one of the shop classes.

_____T_____ **13.** A student had started a (lawn mower) with the gas cap off.

_____I_____ **14.** Gasoline spilled onto the engine and burst into flames.

_____I_____ **15.** The fire spread quickly.

_____T_____ **16.** Some students felt a burning (sensation) in their eyes.

_____T_____ **17.** They heard (sirens) from the street.

_____I_____ **18.** A rescue vehicle arrived at the same time as the fire truck.

_____I_____ **19.** Firefighters hurried into the building.

_____I_____ **20.** The fire was soon extinguished, but by then most of the school

was filled with smoke.

Next Step Some verbs, such as *break, freeze,* and *sing,* can be either transitive or intransitive. Choose one of those verbs and write a sentence using it as a transitive verb. Then write another sentence using it as an intransitive verb.

Verbals

Verbals have split personalities—they are words that are part verb and part noun or adjective or adverb. For example, add *ing* to a verb, and it can become a **gerund**—a verb used as a noun. Or add *ing* or *ed* to a verb, and it can become a **participle**—a verb used as an adjective. Or introduce a verb with the word *to* and it becomes an **infinitive**—a verb used as either a noun, an adjective, or an adverb. (See 730.2–730.4 in *Write Source* for more information.)

Examples

Gerund:

Watching **an expert play is a good way to improve your game**.
("Watching" is used as a noun and the subject of the sentence.)

Participle:

The cat played a watching **game with the** confused **mouse**.
("Watching" and "confused" are used as adjectives. "Watching" modifies "game." "Confused" modifies "mouse.")

Infinitive:

To watch **is** to wait.
("To watch" is the subject and "to wait" is the predicate noun.)

 Directions Underline the verbals in the sentences that follow. In the space below the sentence, name the type of verbal you have found, and explain the job it is doing. There may be more than one verbal in each sentence. The first sentence has been done for you.

1. <u>Smirking</u> at a teacher who scolds you is not wise.

   "Smirking" is a gerund used as the subject of the sentence.

2. <u>Rewarding</u> a dog with treats is a good <u>training</u> technique.

   "Rewarding" is a gerund used as the subject of the sentence. "Training" is a

   participle used as an adjective—it modifies "technique."

3. Trained elephants perform regularly so that they do not become restless.

"Trained" is a participle used as an adjective—it modifies "elephants."

4. I've always dreamed of acting in a broadway musical.

"Acting" is a gerund used as an object of the preposition "of."

5. I would like to fly like a bird.

"To fly" is an infinitive used as the direct object of the sentence.

6. To win the next three games is the team's goal.

"To win" is an infinitive used as the subject of the sentence.

7. In most sports, timing is everything.

"Timing" is a gerund used as the subject of the sentence.

8. Applying for a passport is a good idea even if you don't have immediate

travel plans.

"Applying" is a gerund used as the subject of the sentence.

Next Step Write three sentences following the direction given for each verbal: (1) Use *laughing* as an adjective, (2) use *walking* as a subject, and (3) use *to play* as a direct object. Now label each verbal as either a gerund, a participle, or an infinitive. Share your sentences aloud with a classmate.

Types of Adjectives

There are four special kinds of adjectives. They are demonstrative, compound, indefinite, and predicate. (See 732.4, 732.5, 734.1, and 734.2 in *Write Source* for help with this exercise.)

Directions Each sentence has a different type of adjective underlined. In the space beneath each sentence, identify and then provide an explanation for each type.

1. <u>Some</u> cats enjoy having <u>many</u> mice around.

Type: *Indefinite Adjectives*

Explanation: An ___*indefinite*___ adjective is one that ___*gives an*___ *approximate number or quantity.*

2. <u>This</u> kitten is mean, but <u>that</u> cat is meaner.

Type: *Demonstrative Adjectives*

Explanation: *A demonstrative adjective is one that points out a particular noun.*

3. <u>Scar-faced</u> Bronty is no <u>scaredy-cat</u> guard.

Type: *Compound Adjectives*

Explanation: *A compound adjective is made up of more than one word. (Sometimes it is hyphenated.)*

4. A frustrated kitten is <u>unpleasant</u> and <u>unpredictable</u>.

Type: *Predicate Adjectives*

Explanation: *A predicate adjective is an adjective that follows a linking verb and describes the subject.*

Directions

Use one of the four types of adjectives as one of the central characters in a story. An indefinite adjective, for example, might only think or speak in very general terms. Its favorite phrase might be "Gee, I'm not sure." A demonstrative adjective, on the other hand, might be very bossy. (Ask your teacher if you may work in pairs for this activity.)

_____

_____

_____

_____

_____

_____

_____

_____

_____

_____

_____

_____

_____

_____

_____

Next Step Share your stories in your writing groups or with your class as a whole. Pay special attention to each adjective's personality.

Compound Adjectives

The screen door slams. Three-year-old Adira runs into the kitchen and rummages through cabinets, asking, "Where is my zoo-buggy house?"

I hand my little neighbor the screen-topped "bug zoo" we made for catching fireflies. Adira combines simple words she knows into picture-perfect descriptions without batting an eye.

Compound adjectives—two simple words linked as one compound word—are fun to use and, in informal writing, fun to invent. (See 732.5 in *Write Source* for more information.)

Examples

The fun-loving friends played kickball at the park.
("Kickball" always appears as one word; "fun-loving" doesn't.)

five-dollar **bill**   second-story **office**   40-something **years**
(Numbers combined with words to form compound adjectives are hyphenated.)

The old sock collector paid 50 dollars for hand-knitted argyles.
(Was the collector old? Then write "old sock-collector." Or was he a collector of old socks? If so, write "old-sock collector.")

 Directions Write compound adjectives in the blanks below. The first blank has been done for you. If you need help thinking of compound words, check out the word bank on the next page. *(Answers may vary.)*

1   I will never forget the crazy, _____*goofed-up*_____ Halloween party my

2   sister and I threw for our _____*seventh-grade*_____ friends. When the

3   _____*30-some*_____ kids started arriving around 6:00 p.m., things

4   looked normal. Within hours, though, everything changed.

5   We had the party in our _____*cleaned-up*_____ barn. There was just one

6   _____*teeny-weeny*_____ problem: my sister's _____*bullheaded*_____ donkey.

7   George, the donkey, doesn't move out of his _____*straw-stuffed*_____ stall

8   unless it is his idea. So our _____*half-baked*_____ plan was to include him in

9   the party. George would be a steed in _____*tinfoil*_____ armor. Instead of

10   bobbing for apples, our _____*fun-loving*_____ guests would hop on George and

11   ride toward a _____*pumpkin-head*_____ scarecrow. The winner would have to knock

12   the scarecrow's _____*oversized*_____ head off with a _____*lambs-wool*_____

13   duster. It sounded simple.

14   We didn't anticipate George's _____*so-called*_____ enthusiasm for acting.

15   Instead of aiming for the scarecrow, George headed for the _____*well-decorated*_____

16   refreshment table. As he slammed into the sawhorses supporting the

17   tabletop, soda pop cans burst and sprayed sticky fountains at the

18   _____*overhead*_____ lights. The lights went out.

19   Shrieking kids crowded toward the door of the _____*blacked-out*_____ .

20   barn. There, they ran smack into a _____*snaggletoothed*_____ phantom with

21   burning eyes! Was it a _____*fire-breathing*_____ monster? Nope. It was our

22   _____*lawn-mower*_____ tractor covered with _____*glow-in-the-dark*_____ paint!

goofed-up	happy-go-lucky	bullheaded	straw-stuffed	blacked-out
glow-in-the-dark	seventh-grade	30-some	cleaned-up	fire-breathing
overhead	so-called	pumpkin-head	makeshift	teeny-weeny
lawn-mower	well-decorated	tinfoil	lambs-wool	warm-up
snaggletoothed	oversized	half-baked	fun-loving	noise-making

Predicate Adjectives

You know that an adjective tells something special about a noun. The noun a predicate adjective describes is always the subject of a sentence or a clause. Predicate adjectives are easy to spot, too, because they always follow a linking verb.

"Wait a minute," you're thinking. "Predicate nouns follow linking verbs, too!" Indeed, they do—but predicate nouns rename the subject instead of describing it. (See 734.2 in *Write Source* for more information.)

Examples

Predicate Adjective:

The future is **predictable in science fiction.**

(The verb "is" links the subject noun "future" to its predicate adjective "predictable.")

Predicate Noun:

Aliens is **a science-fiction movie about the future.**

(The verb "is" links the subject "*Aliens*" to the predicate noun "movie.")

Note: Most **linking verbs** are forms of the verb *be—am, is, are, was, were, be, being, been.* Other verbs—*smell, feel, look, taste, remain, appear, sound, seem, become, grow, stand,* and *turn*—may also do the job of linking a subject to a predicate noun or a predicate adjective. Some words may be used as both linking verbs and action verbs. How the verb functions in a *particular* sentence is the key to whether it is a linking verb or an action verb.

 Directions

In the sentences below, underline the subject once and the verb twice. Then label each bold-faced word: "PA" for predicate adjective or "PN" for predicate noun. The first one has been done for you.

1. People are **curious** about finding new ways to build houses. `PA`

2. A house may not look any **different** from its neighbor, but its building blocks `PA`

   may be **extraordinary!** `PA`

3. Straw-bale houses are grand **properties** or simple **huts.** `PN` `PN`

4. The laziest one of the *Three Little Pigs* was not the first **builder** to decide `PN`

   that straw is an excellent construction **material.** `PN`

5. Houses of compacted straw coated with clay <u>were</u> **common** *PA* in ancient Asia and Europe.

6. A one-room <u>schoolhouse</u> built in 1886 near Bayard, Nebraska, <u>is</u> the first recorded **building** *PN* made of rectangular bales.

7. An <u>article</u> in a book titled *Shelter* <u>is</u> **responsible** *PA* for renewed interest in straw-bale building.

8. Straw <u>houses</u> coated with stucco, plaster, or clay <u>look</u> **beautiful** *PA* and <u>are</u> very **strong.** *PA*

9. The <u>houses</u> <u>are</u> unusually **well-insulated.** *PA*

10. <u>Straw</u> <u>is</u> an abundant and a renewable **resource.** *PN*

11. <u>Air</u> in a straw house <u>is</u> generally **free** *PA* of fumes and pollutants.

12. <u>Building</u> with bales <u>is</u> **speedy;** *PA* <u>walls</u> <u>can be erected</u> in one weekend.

13. <u>Houses</u> built of straw <u>are</u> still **rare** *PA*—but <u>they</u> <u>can be found</u> from the United States to Russia, and from France to Nova Scotia and Mexico.

Next Step Read about other unusual kinds of houses in other books at your library. Let your imagination run wild! Write a description of your ideal house. Use some colorful predicate adjectives.

Forms of Adjectives

An adjective is used to describe a noun or a pronoun—"the *small* TV." An adjective can even go one step further when it is used in a comparison—"the TV is *smaller* than your fist." Each adjective has three forms of comparison: *positive, comparative*, and *superlative*. (See the examples below and 734.3–734.5 in *Write Source* for more information.)

Examples

Positive:

Frozen yogurt is a light dessert. It is delicious.
(The *positive form* of an adjective describes a noun or a pronoun without comparing it to anyone or anything else.)

Comparative:

Frozen yogurt is a lighter dessert than ice cream.
Frozen yogurt is more delicious than ice cream.
(The *comparative form* of an adjective [adjective + *er*] compares two nouns or pronouns. Most adjectives of two or more syllables use the modifier "more," instead of adding *er,* to show the comparison.)

Superlative:

Frozen yogurt is the lightest dessert of the five on this menu.
Frozen yogurt is the most delicious dessert I can think of.
(The *superlative form* of an adjective [adjective + *est*] compares three or more nouns or pronouns. Most adjectives of two or more syllables use the modifier "most," instead of adding *est,* to show the comparison.)

Note: A few adjectives are irregular (*good, better, best* and *little, less, least*).

 Directions Use each of the following adjectives in a sentence. Use the adjective in the form indicated in parentheses. The first one has been done for you.

tall   1. At 20,320 feet, Mt. McKinley is _____*tall*_____ , while South
                                                        (positive)

America's Mt. Aconcagua is even _____*taller*_____ , but Mt.
                                         (comparative)

Everest is the _____*tallest*_____ .
                      (superlative)

old   2. Evan, born at 11:59 p.m. on July 3, is a day ___*older*___ than
                 (comparative)

                 his twin brother, born at 12:04 a.m. on July 4.

funny   3. Who is the ___*funniest*___ comedian on television?
                 (superlative)

good   4. I am good at all of the "extreme-B" sports—boards, blades, and

                 BMX biking—but I am ___*best*___ at snowboarding.
                 (superlative)

charming 5. The only quality my mom finds ___*more charming*___ in a
                 (comparative)

                 daughter than whining is the ability to burp on command.

good   6. You can buy many types of tires for a road bike, but for traction

                 on dry pavement, the ___*best*___ tire has no tread, so its
                 (superlative)

                 surface is totally in contact with the road.

comfortable 7. My dad's recliner is really ugly, but it is ___*more comfortable*___
                 (comparative)

                 than my mom's rocking chair.

boring   8. That picnic was so ___*boring*___ that even the mosquitoes
                 (positive)

                 fell asleep, but it was not the ___*most boring*___ picnic I've
                 (superlative)

                 ever attended.

bad   9. My brother got a ___*bad*___ grade in ninth-grade
                 (positive)

                 algebra, but my grade was ___*worse*___ .
                 (comparative)

Next Step As you completed the activity above, you probably noticed that some adjectives like *bad, worse,* and *worst* are irregular. Compare notes with your classmates and see how many irregular adjectives you can think of.

Adverbs

Adverbs are used to modify verbs, adjectives, or other adverbs. There are four basic types of adverbs: *adverbs of time, place, manner,* and *degree.* (See page 736 in *Write Source* for more information.)

> **Directions** Circle 11 adverbs in the following sentences. The first sentence has been done for you.

1. Lightning streaked (continuously,) driving jagged spears into the dark night.

2. John's mother (hesitantly) and (shakily) agreed that the lightning was pretty.

3. Four-year-old John found the whole experience (quite) exciting.

4. (Suddenly,) they were plunged into darkness.

5. To move in the dark was (very) difficult, but they (slowly) managed to find their way.

6. The first thing that they spotted was a (brightly) flashing red light.

7. Cars were moving (slowly) as they approached the corner.

8. John and his mother walked (cautiously) across the street.

9. They stepped (carefully) onto the curb.

10. John and his mother will (never) forget that experience.

Next Step Write four more adverbs on the lines below. Then use all five adverbs in sentences in a very short story.

_____*especially*_____   _____   _____

_____   _____   _____

Directions

In the space below, write a descriptive paragraph about drivers of cars or motorcycles and how they maneuver through traffic. Use each of the listed adverbs in the paragraph.

well   fast   quickly   often   entirely

Forms of Adverbs

An adverb is a word that tells us more about a verb, an adjective, or another adverb. Adverbs usually explain *how, when, where,* or *to what extent (how often, how long, how much)* something happened.

They have three forms: positive, comparative, and superlative. The positive form modifies another word without making a comparison. (See 738.2–738.4 in *Write Source* for more information.)

Examples

Positive:

Performing fleas train vigorously.

("Vigorously" modifies the verb "train" without making any comparisons.)

Comparative:

Jumping frogs train more vigorously **than performing fleas.**

("More vigorously" modifies the verb "train" and compares how "frogs" train to how "fleas" train.)

Superlative:

Fido's flea is the most vigorously **trained insect in the world.**

("Most vigorously" modifies the adjective "trained" and compares one "flea" to all other insects.)

 Directions   Use each of the following words as an adverb in a sentence. (Use the adverb in the form indicated in parentheses.) The first one has been done for you.

bad   **1.** When the teacher stepped out of the room, the students behaved

_____*badly*_____ .
      (positive)

clear   **2.** Greg speaks _____*more clearly*_____ than Ann, his opponent
              (comparative)

for student council.

fast   **3.** Who ran _____*fastest*_____ in the relay?
          (superlative)

gentle   **4.** She _____*gently*_____ stroked the frightened dog.
        (positive)

noisy   **5.** Mark my words, this discussion began quietly, but it will end

            noisily
            _____.
            (positive)

careful   **6.** Lock the door ___*carefully*___ — ___*more carefully*___
                            (positive)   *(comparative)*

         than you have ever done it before!

loud   **7.** Marshmallow Man from *Ghostbusters* stomps around

            loudly
            _____.
            (positive)

quick   **8.** He won the pancake-eating contest by floating the flapjacks in

         milk and gulping them ___*most quickly*___.
                                 (superlative)

sincere   **9.** Think carefully about the questions, and answer them

            sincerely
            _____.
            (positive)

stylish   **10.** The '57 Thunderbird sports car was designed ___*more stylishly*___
                                                 (comparative)

         than that year's Chevy Corvette model, but the Chevy has become

         a legend.

well   **11.** Picabo Street skied ___*best*___ in the 1998 Winter Olympics,
                              (superlative)

         even though she was recovering from a serious injury.

slow   **12.** Please drive ___*slow (or) slowly*___!
                         (positive)

Next Step Now you try it! Write three sentences about a game or contest. Write one sentence in which you use one adverb in the positive form, one in the comparative form, and one in the superlative form.

Conjunctive Adverbs

A **conjunctive adverb** is an adverb that connects two clauses. Conjunctive adverbs show relationships between two ideas, such as cause and effect, sequence, and comparison. (For more information, see 738.1 in *Write Source*.)

Examples

On our trip to New York City we'll visit the Statute of Liberty; <u>also</u>, we'll go to the Empire State Building.

It's beginning to rain; <u>therefore</u>, the ball game is cancelled for today.

Ming is a hard worker; <u>on the other hand</u>, at times she can be lazy.

 Directions Underline the conjunctive adverb or phrase in each sentence or pair of sentences. The first one has been done for you.

1. The old house down the street has been empty for years; <u>therefore</u>, people in the neighborhood thought it was scary.

2. Rita and Laura were afraid of the house; <u>nevertheless</u>, they decided to investigate it.

3. They stood on the doorstep for ten minutes; <u>finally</u>, they opened the door and went in.

4. The house smelled old and stale; <u>furthermore</u>, there were cobwebs clinging to the furniture.

5. They wanted to leave; <u>however</u>, their curiosity wouldn't let them.

6. Suddenly they heard a door creak open; <u>then</u>, there were strange noises coming closer and closer.

7. A dark shadow slid across the floor; <u>consequently</u>, both girls screamed.

8. A large black cat appeared in the corner; <u>now</u>, the girls knew exactly what had made the noises.

Next Step Write a short speech on a favorite topic you know a lot about. Use at least four conjunctive adverbs to transition from one idea to another. Be sure to use correct punctuation. When you are finished, deliver your speech to the class.

Prepositions

Prepositions such as *at, about, by, for, in, of, on,* and *to,* among others, have been used in our language for well over 1,400 years. Prepositions are words that show position or direction. They also introduce prepositional phrases.

Prepositional phrases are an indispensable part of our language. (*Indispensabl*e means we can't do without them.) Just think how sentences, such as the examples below, would read without the prepositional phrases. There wouldn't be much left, would there? (See page 742 in *Write Source* for more information.)

Examples

Prepositional Phrases:

Write every day in a personal journal.

Begin writing with a particular idea in mind.

 Directions   Underline all of the prepositional phrases in the journal entry below. *Caution:* Do not underline infinitives (the word "to" followed by a verb) as prepositional phrases! The first one has been done for you.

1   April 12

2   I was late for my guitar lesson tonight. Usually, I'm at the studio

3   by 6:30, but I was late because of my cat Tom. He ran away

4   during last night's storm. I looked everywhere for him.

5   I looked in the garage because there are lots of little niches in there.

6   I looked in the laundry room because cats usually like to curl up

7   in warm, soft places. I finally headed outside and even looked in the trees.

8   Tom just wasn't to be found, so I stopped looking. After supper, I heard a

9   purr in my room. Leave it to a cat to be unpredictable. I found Tom

10   under the bed.

Directions Rewrite the following sentences so that each begins with a prepositional phrase. Place a comma after the phrase if you think one is needed to make the meaning of the sentence clear. The first one has been done for you.

1. Dogs are often used as companions in modern nursing homes.

   In modern nursing homes, dogs are often used as companions.

2. Many people in nursing homes think of the resident dog as their very own pet.

   In nursing homes, many of the people think of the resident dog as their very own pet.

3. Some residents leave out special treats for the dog's daily visit.

   For the dog's daily visit, some residents leave out special treats.

4. Golden retrievers are suitable pets according to some staff members.

   According to some staff members, golden retrievers are suitable pets.

5. The nurses usually walk the dogs between shifts.

   Between shifts, the nurses usually walk the dogs.

Next Step Write a story starter, similar to the one below, using a two-word preposition from the list on page 742 in *Write Source*. Share your story starter with a partner.

Together with her friend, Elisha was a curious young lady.
One foggy September evening, her curiosity led to . . .

Prepositional Phrases and Subject-Verb Agreement

A **prepositional phrase** is a group of words that begins with a preposition and includes a noun or pronoun, which is known as *the object of the preposition*. When a prepositional phrase is placed between a subject and a verb, it can cause confusion with subject-verb agreement. The main subject—and not the noun or pronoun in the phrase—determines subject-verb agreement.

Examples

Correct: **The house with four bedrooms is up for sale.**

Incorrect: **The house with four bedrooms are up for sale.**

Correct: **The colors of the painting are vivid.**

Incorrect: **The colors of the painting is vivid.**

 Directions   Read each sentence with a prepositional phrase. If the subject-verb agreement is correct, write C in the blank. If it is incorrect, write I in the blank and rewrite the sentence correctly. The first one has been done for you.

_____*I*_____   **1.** The stories featured on the evening newscast is mostly

depressing.

The stories featured on the evening newscast are mostly

depressing.

_____*C*_____   **2.** The bus with twenty passengers was coming down the hill.

_____

_____*I*_____   **3.** The book under the magazines were hidden from view.

The book under the magazines was hidden from view.

_C_   **4.** The firefighters from the downtown station put out the blaze.

_____

_I_   **5.** The restaurants in the shopping mall serves our community well.

    The restaurants in the shopping mall serve our community well.

_____

_I_   **6.** The litter of six puppies play with the child.

    The litter of six puppies plays with the child.

_I_   **7.** The speeches of the leading actor runs many pages.

    The speeches of the leading actor run many pages.

_C_   **8.** The cave of the brown bats attracts many visitors.

_____

Next Step Write four sentences containing prepositional phrases. Make sure the subject-verb agreement in your sentences is correct. Read your sentences aloud to a partner.

Interjections

An interjection is a word or phrase used to express strong emotion or surprise. *Wow!* and *Yikes!* are interjections. A comma or an exclamation point is usually used to separate the interjection from the rest of the sentence. (See page 746 in *Write Source* for more information.)

Directions Underline each interjection in the sentences that follow. The first one has been done for you.

1. "<u>Hey</u>, Joe, guess where I'm going next week?"

2. "<u>Well</u>, let's see," answered Joe. "To Australia? Siberia? The moon?"

3. "<u>Okay</u>, enough of the wise-guy routine. I'm going scuba diving."

4. "<u>Cool</u>. Do you get to use air tanks and all that?" asked Joe.

5. "<u>Yep</u>, and we get to explore a coral reef and a couple of shipwrecks."

6. "<u>Holy mackerel</u>! That sounds like a great time. Do you need someone to carry your flippers or something?" asked Joe, drooling.

7. "<u>Oops</u>, I forgot to sign up for flippers. Thanks for reminding me."

8. "What kind of creatures do you expect to see? I mean, <u>whoa</u>, you better stay away from the sharks, barracudas, and octopuses," warned Joe.

9. "<u>Yeah</u>, I'll keep my distance. <u>Hmmm</u>, maybe I should buy some shark repellent or something."

10. "<u>Nah</u>," Joe laughed. "No shark is going to be interested in someone as tasteless as you!"

> **Directions**
>
> On the lines below, write your own dialogue about an adventure you've had (or would like to have). Use interjections whenever they seem right. If they are used well, interjections will make your dialogue sound much more real.

_____

_____

_____

_____

_____

_____

_____

_____

_____

_____

_____

_____

_____

_____

_____

_____

_____

_____

Subordinating Conjunctions

Subordinating conjunctions connect clauses to form complex sentences. The resulting sentences often carry more meaning than the shorter independent clauses and also help to make your writing read more smoothly. (See 746.1 in *Write Source* for more information.)

Examples

Two Sentences:

Martha entered a 124-mile ice-skating race. She felt ready for it.

A Compound Sentence:

Martha entered a 124-mile ice-skating race, and she felt ready for it.
(A comma and the coordinating conjunction "and" connect the two sentences.)

A Complex Sentence:

Martha entered a 124-mile ice-skating race because she felt ready for it.
(The subordinating conjunction "because" connects the two sentences.)

 Directions Subordinating conjunctions connect two ideas to form meaningful complex sentences. Some subordinating conjunctions express time (*before*), some express the reason why (*because*), and some serve as conditional words (*unless*). In each sentence, circle the subordinating conjunctions. Put the group of words (or clause) each conjunction introduces in parentheses. The first one has been done for you.

1. For his own safety, a soccer referee in Greece disguised himself as a priest after a match (because) (he had greatly upset the local fans).

2. Alex Wickham must have had a lot of confidence (since) (he dove from a rocky cliff the height of a 20-story building).

3. He lost consciousness (before) (he hit the water).

4. (Although) (he survived the dive), his body was all black-and-blue.

5. Two tennis players once continued a point for 78 straight minutes (until) (one player had to stop the volley to give a tennis lesson).

6. (When) (Lawson Robertson and Harry Hillman set a track-and-field record), they did it in a three-legged race.

7. (Although) (he had a 150-pound man on his back), Noah Young ran a mile in 8 minutes 30 seconds.

8. (While) (Ernest Mensen ran a distance of 1,960 miles), he ate only biscuits covered with raspberry syrup.

9. Ernest Mensen saved time (when) (he ran) (because) (he knew how to find shortcuts through forests).

10. The modern marathon race got its name from the plain of Marathon in Greece (where) (an ancient battle took place).

11. (When) (a man named Philippedes ran from Marathon to Athens), he delivered the news of a Greek victory over Persia.

12. (Because) (the first marathon was 26 miles), the modern marathon race during the Olympic Games is also 26 miles.

Next Step Write a paragraph about a cooking, camping, or classroom experience. Use short, simple sentences as if you were just learning to read and write. Then exchange paragraphs with a classmate and revise each other's work. Try to use some subordinate conjunctions in your revisions. Share your revised paragraph with a classmate.

Coordinating and Correlative Conjunctions

The place two roads come together is called a *junction*. A similar word *conjunction* is the name of the part of speech that joins things—other words, phrases, or clauses. There are three types of conjunctions. This exercise will look at two of the three types: coordinating and correlative. **Coordinating conjunctions** always connect two equal sentence elements of the same kind—a word to a word, a phrase to a phrase, or a clause to a clause. **Correlative conjunctions,** like coordinating conjunctions, connect elements of the same kind, but correlative conjunctions are used in pairs. (See page 744 in *Write Source* for more information.)

Examples

Coordinating Conjunction:

Mathematics and **music communicate without language.**
(The coordinating conjunction "and" connects two words—"mathematics" and "music.")

Correlative Conjunction:

Choose either **music** or **art as your elective class.**
(The correlative conjunctions "either," "or" connect two words—"music" and "art.")

 Directions Join each pair of sentences that follow using coordinating or correlative conjunctions. You may delete words and move words around. The first sentence has been done for you. *(Answers may vary.)*

1. I would like to visit Iceland. I would also like to visit Greenland.

I would like to visit Iceland and Greenland.

2. In high school, I want to try out for track. I also want to try out for basketball.

In high school, I want to try out for track and basketball.

3. Many athletes want to play two sports. The seasons have to be at different times.

Many athletes want to play two sports, but the seasons have to be at

different times.

4. In some places football and soccer have the same season. A student must choose one sport or the other.

In some places football and soccer have the same season, so a

student must choose one sport or the other.

5. My brother could not decide which sport to play. He had to choose football or soccer.

My brother could not decide whether to play football or to play soccer.

6. He enjoys both sports. He's pretty good at football and soccer.

He enjoys both football and soccer, and he's pretty good at both

sports.

7. He finally chose football. He was happy to have made a decision.

He finally chose football and was happy to have made a decision.

8. He was unhappy about missing his friends on the soccer team. He also thought he would miss the constant movement and pace of a soccer game.

He was unhappy not only about missing his friends on the soccer

team but also about missing the constant movement and pace of

a soccer game.

9. Now he talks about football all the time. We used to talk together about both soccer and football.

We used to talk together about both soccer and football, but now he

talks about football all the time.

Parts of Speech Review 1

In the English language there are eight parts of speech. They help you understand words and how to use them. Every word in every sentence is a part of speech.

Directions Write one of the eight parts of speech under each of the eight faces. If you need help, turn to page 748 in *Write Source*. Then write a sentence that uses that part of speech on the blank beside the face. Circle the word. *(Answers will vary.)*

1. *noun* — The (boy) smiled.

2. *conjunction* — Fred finished his math (and) science.

3. *preposition* — Kate tossed a penny (in) the fountain.

4. *pronoun* — Jess said the hat was (his.)

5. *adjective* — Antoine lifted the (heavy) box.

6. *verb* — Janey (jogged) five miles.

7. *adverb* — Jermaine (carefully) crossed the icy walk.

8. *interjection* — Becky shouted, ("Wow!")

> **Directions** Identify the part of speech for each underlined word. Find five examples of each part of speech, except for the interjection, which has only one example. (Look at page 748 in *Write Source*.)

nouns ☐ ☐ ☐ ☐ ☐   adverbs ☐ ☐ ☐ ☐ ☐   conjunctions ☐ ☐ ☐ ☐ ☐

verbs ☐ ☐ ☐ ☐ ☐   adjectives ☐ ☐ ☐ ☐ ☐   interjection ☐

pronouns ☐ ☐ ☐ ☐ ☐   prepositions ☐ ☐ ☐ ☐ ☐

1   In the summer after eighth grade, Rene took *(verb)* a bus from *(preposition)* Vermont to

2   her uncle's cottage in New Jersey. Her "graduation *(adjective)* present" turned out to be a

3   crash *(adjective)* course in the school of life.

4   At a stop in New York City, she visited a newsstand. Suddenly, *(adverb)* someone

5   snatched her purse. She never *(adverb)* saw the thief. Her ticket and *(conjunction)* her money were

6   gone. She patted her side as if *(conjunction)* the bag would reappear. Anger overwhelmed *(verb)*

7   her. Oh, *(interjection)* how could someone *(pronoun)* be so evil? How would she get to Ocean City now?

8   Fortunately, the bus driver let her call her parents. They *(pronoun)* told her about *(preposition)*

9   Western Union, the nationwide *(adjective)* telegraph network. Her parents promised to

10   wire money to the nearest agent. *(noun)*

11   Hiking through *(preposition)* downtown Manhattan, she composed *(verb)* herself. *(pronoun)* In high

12   school, she would *(verb)* write a fine story about her adventure. In the cramped *(adjective)*

13   Western Union office, she studied people with *(preposition)* a writer's eye. *(noun)* They looked

14   tired *(adjective)* and afraid. Everyone *(pronoun)* there had a problem. *(noun)* But when *(conjunction)* a man beside her

15   in *(preposition)* a tie-dyed T-shirt started to whistle, everybody laughed. They became *(verb)* a kind

16   of family.

17   Later, *(adverb)* while *(conjunction)* she was sunning herself on the Jersey shore, she decided

18   her story would not *(adverb)* be about crime. It would be about the feelings *(noun)* and *(conjunction)*

19   experiences that *(pronoun)* draw people together. *(adverb)*

Parts of Speech Review 2

Directions Unscramble the words below to name the eight parts of speech.

1. unno _____noun_____ (6)   5. tadviejec _____adjective_____ (6)

2. berv _____verb_____ (6)   6. brevda _____adverb_____ (6)

3. spotiperion _____preposition_____ (6)   7. junconontic _____conjunction_____ (6)

4. ropnoun _____pronoun_____ (6)   8. jecretnition _____interjection_____ (1)

Directions Identify the part of speech for each underlined word. The number after each scrambled word above tells you how many examples of that part of speech are underlined in the exercise. (See page 748 in *Write Source*.)

1   You would <u>recognize</u> *(verb)* Robin Williams or Danny DeVito <u>on</u> *(preposition)* TV. But

2   would you recognize a picture of the most <u>famous</u> *(adjective)* cartoon-voice actor in

3   history, the man who created over 500 different voices?

4   The man <u>with</u> *(preposition)* the rubber voice was <u>Mel Blanc</u> *(noun)*. You <u>know</u> *(verb)* him as Bugs

5   Bunny and Foghorn Leghorn, as Yosemite Sam <u>and</u> *(conjunction)* the Tasmanian Devil,

6   as Fred Flintstone and Porky Pig—to name just a few of the hundreds

7   of <u>characters</u> *(noun)* he created <u>for</u> *(preposition)* Warner Brothers. During the glory days of

8   radio, Blanc performed <u>weekly</u> *(adverb)* in 18 transcontinental radio shows. He also

9   <u>commanded</u> *(verb)* top pay when recording for <u>rival</u> *(adjective)* companies, once earning $800

10   for Gideon the Cat's hiccup in the Disney movie *Pinocchio*. (At the time,

11   other cartoon actors were earning a mere $50 a day.)

12   Blanc started his <u>career</u> *(noun)* as a musician and bandleader. <u>Luckily</u> *(adverb)* for <u>us</u> *(pronoun)*,

13   one evening in the 1930s he was asked to host a talent show in Portland,

14 Oregon. A blizzard forced the contestants to stay home.

15   Blanc decided to do the entire show _himself_! He _cleverly_ created a
        (pronoun)   (adverb)

16 voice for each of the "contestants"—a yodeler, a violinist, and a hillbilly—and

17 faked interviews with _them_, using his "_real_" voice as the interviewer. The
                         (pronoun)   (adjective)

18 audience loved him.

19   After his surprising success, Blanc headed for Hollywood. Getting

20 an audition _with_ a cartoon company was not easy. For a year and a half,
                (preposition)

21 Warner Brothers refused to hear him. His lucky _break_ came _when_ the
                                                   (noun)   (conjunction)

22 studio _needed_ a new voice for a drunken bull.
           (verb)

23   About that time, Warner Brothers was developing the character of a

24 _timid_ little pig. When Blanc was asked in a interview _if_ he had lived on a
    (adjective)   (conjunction)

25 farm, he _replied_, "_No_, but I went out to a pig farm _and_ wallowed around for
             (verb)   (interjection)   (conjunction)

26 a couple of weeks." _That_ is how Porky Pig got his voice.
                        (pronoun)

27   _Around_ that time, Bugs Hardaway was developing another new
        (preposition)

28 character. _He_ described Happy Rabbit as little, tough, and a real stinker.
               (pronoun)

29 Mel Blanc _thoughtfully_ remarked that the _toughest_ voice in the United
              (adverb)   (adjective)

30 States had to be from the _Bronx_ or Brooklyn. Blanc _easily_ combined the
                              (noun)   (adverb)

31 New York _accents_ and then suggested that Happy Rabbit's name should be
             (noun)

32 changed to honor his creator. Thus, Bugs Bunny was born.

33 Sylvester the Cat got a _very_ slurpy sounding voice _because_ he is a
                            (adverb)   (conjunction)

34 _sloppy-looking_ cat. Daffy Duck's voice is a lot like Sylvester's _but_ was
    (adjective)   (conjunction)

35 recorded _at_ a different speed. Because he is tiny, Tweety got a baby voice.
             (preposition)

36 Even Woody Woodpecker, _who_ was performed by Walter Lanz, _owes_ his
                          (pronoun)   (verb)

37 trademark laugh to Mel Blanc.